KICKBOXING
FROM BEGINNER TO BLACK BELT

KICKBOXING
FROM BEGINNER TO BLACK BELT

Justyn Billingham

THE CROWOOD PRESS

First published in 2008 by
The Crowood Press Ltd
Ramsbury, Marlborough
Wiltshire SN8 2HR

www.crowood.com

British Library Cataloguing-in-Publication Data
A catalogue record for this book is available from the British Library.

ISBN 978 1 84797 037 4

Disclaimer
Please note that the author and the publisher of this book are not responsible in any manner whatsoever for any damage or injury of any kind that may result from practising, or applying, the principles, ideas, techniques and/or following the instructions/information described in this publication. Since the physical activities described in this book may be too strenuous in nature for some readers to engage in safely, it is essential that a doctor be consulted before undertaking training.

Typeset and designed by D & N Publishing
Lambourn Woodlands, Hungerford, Berkshire.

Printed and bound in Malaysia by Times Offset (M) Sdn Bhd.

Dedication

I would like to dedicate my very first book to my two children Harley and Isabella who, like the martial arts, have helped change my life.

Acknowledgements

A lot of people helped me to write this book, so I feel it's only right to thank everyone that was either directly or indirectly involved in some way. My past and present instructors in the martial arts, without whom I certainly wouldn't have written this book. Ian Healey for his design skill and his patience. Natalie Britchford for her expert knowledge of the human body. My very good friend Nigel Sleath for more than just his appearance in this book but for all the help, support and guidance he has given me over the years, and finally to my wife Sam for being my rock and putting up with so much. I couldn't have done it without your help and support.

Contents

Foreword

During the time that I have known Justyn Billingham he has done a great deal to promote the fine art of kickboxing, both as a teacher and a former competitor.

During his years of training, research and teaching he has studied with teachers of the highest calibre, and throughout his competitive years Justyn had numerous opportunities to test his art in actual use. This makes him something of a rarity in present day martial arts – especially in dojos and academies, where theory is often loudly heard while actual practice sits quietly in the corner.

Now we are fortunate that he is sharing his vast knowledge and skill with a new generation of kickboxers. This book advances our knowledge of this remarkable martial art and I hope that it will introduce would-be kickboxers all over the world to the amazing kicking techniques of Justyn Billingham.

Bob Sykes
(Editor of *Martial Arts Illustrated Magazine*)

1 Introduction

As I sit here in my home office writing the introduction for this, my very first book, I glance over to the wall of certificates prominently displayed before me. There are not many things I keep on show from my past, as most of it has been boxed up and put in the loft to make way for the more important clutter that comes from running several martial arts schools and sharing a house with two young children. But I'm quite proud of my certificates, particularly my very first white belt one, as they are a constant reminder of where I have come from and the huge amount of time, dedication, money and hard work that has been invested to achieve those bits of paper.

Much to the amazement of people that get to see these certificates, it's actually my white belt one that takes pride of place. Issued by the Tae kwon do Association of Great Britain (TAGB) on the 22 July 1986 and signed by my instructor at the time, Ian Ferguson, and the examiner for my very first ever grading, the highly respected Paul Donnelly, it sits surrounded by my many other dan certificates, which almost seem a little surreal now – particularly as my first one is dated 24 July 1990, over seventeen years ago. Nevertheless, I find them good motivational tools from an era that was hugely responsible in shaping my life into what it is today.

The irony of it all is I never really planned to study a martial art. I used to love watching martial-art films and would regularly kick and punch my way round the house afterwards (normally quite badly), but had I not experienced something that would change my life forever, I think this is probably the nearest I would have ever got.

As my parents divorced when I was five, I was brought up by my mother. A very loving and caring parent, she amazed me when she agreed to let me go to France for a daytrip with some friends.

Some of the dads had hired a coach and along with their friends, planned to stock it up with beer from the hypermarkets in Boulogne and drive straight back again. My six friends and I thought it would be pretty cool to tag along for the ride, so we badgered the dads into letting us go.

As soon as the coach reached its destination, the dads started loading the coach, and my friends and I started exploring, excited by the fact that we were on foreign land. As we neared the town, two of the local residents, who, I would guess, were around eighteen years old, approached me and, in broken English, asked me for money. I politely explained that I didn't have any and attempted to walk off and re-join my friends who were waiting for me down the road; however, the two youths obviously didn't believe me and pulled me back.

They asked once more and when I again failed to hand over any money they decided to take it out on my face, punching, kicking and head butting me, before finally spraying me in the face with some kind of anti-mugging spray. I was actually quite relieved to get sprayed in the face as I honestly thought that one of the youths was going to pull out a knife instead. Almost as soon as it had begun it was over and the next thing I remember I was being helped up off the floor by my friends, who had watched the whole thing from down the road, along with the many adults that were passing by at the time. As I was unable to see for the rest of the trip and no one wanted to stop off at a French hospital, I had to endure the coach journey back to England and receive treatment almost twenty-four hours later. It was then I decided to start a martial art.

As somebody who appreciates a good kick, I feel that I was fortunate enough to study tae kwon do as my first martial art, under the expert tuition of Ian Ferguson. Although as a teenager I found the discipline hard and the patterns boring, Ian was a great motivator and his ability to get the best out of me helped to cement my future in the martial-arts world. Were it not for Ian, I'm sure I would have joined the ranks of all the other martial-art quitters, many years ago.

I remember spending hours at tae kwon do tournaments after my fights in the coloured belt sections were over, waiting for the black belt categories to start, just so I could watch these incredible fighters perform amazing spinning and jumping kicks, and I remember thinking to myself at the time, 'I wish I could do that'. As I got more and more into my training, I started to discover something else was also developing as well as my physical skills – my self confidence. Having always been quite bad at sport as a kid, I actually began believing that if I put my mind to it, I could actually achieve the incredible levels I had been so used to watching only the best achieve; so I upped my training from twice a week to five nights a week and began to embark on a serious stretching and flexibility programme that still continues to this very day.

It soon became apparent to me that the harder I trained, the better I became, and the more I worked on my flexibility, the easier I found the kicks. Common sense really, but from my experiences as a martial arts instructor, not something that everybody gets. I still feel now, as I did then, that this was the secret formula anyone first starting a martial art is looking for, and the reason that people quit is because they either don't find it or they don't like the secret when they do find it. From then on it was a simple case of the harder I trained, the better I became, until such time that, as a teenager and one of the youngest and smallest students in an advanced class of fully grown adults, I soon began out-kicking and beating the higher grades. I felt I needed more...

Whilst studying tae kwon do, I also joined a local karate school run by Sensei John Kane. John Kane was quite a pioneer in his day and his revolutionary approach to the martial arts helped to build up one of the biggest full-time schools in the area. At its peak we had students travelling over a hundred miles to train with us on a weekly basis, due to our success on the tournament circuits.

As the eighties moved into the nineties, 'freestyle' started to become the buzz word of the time and the school broke away from its karate roots and started focusing more on kickboxing. Each to their own, I always say, but this change in approach suited me much better as it no longer meant kata or standing in line punching and kicking the air for hours at a time, which I really did not enjoy. All of a sudden we were working with focus pads, kick shields, punch bags, floor-to-ceiling balls, speedballs and doing hours of sparring and conditioning drills. When we weren't training, we were fighting, and every Sunday we would take a 52-seater coach journey somewhere in the country to fight at one tournament or another. The coach was also a necessity as it was the only vehicle large enough to cope with all the trophies we would bring back.

These were the days when it was commonplace for kids to train alongside adults and John's school had a huge number of loyal junior students. For the next ten years, or thereabouts, I would train and fight alongside many junior students, such as Matt Winsper, James Winsper and Drew Neal, who had a huge following as junior fighters and have since gone on to become world champions and incredible martial artists in their own right. Although sadly it no longer exists, Kippo's Academy of Karate and Kickboxing was responsible for producing some of the greatest fighters in the country, as well as some equally great instructors, and thanks to the friends that I made throughout my many years training at this school, it is a time of my life that I shall never forget.

From here I started training with Steve Winsper, who had decided to start his own kickboxing school, opening his first one in Halesowen. As one of the greatest coaches I have ever known, Steve's enthusiasm, dedication and ability to get the best out of anyone, helped to raise my level even further and it wasn't very long before Steve was turning out some good fighters and his school was starting to grow. As Steve was only teaching twice a week at this early time in his career, I decided to start training with Dave Kane, John Kane's younger brother. Dave ran a school on the other side of town and, although we had had a run-in at a tournament some years previously (I had cost his fighter the fight by awarding the deciding point to the other guy – a genuine decision, although not always seen that way by the losing team!), I had the utmost respect for Dave; so I decided to pay him a visit and see if I could start training with him.

Dave welcomed me into his school and before long I began teaching some of the classes for him. This was my first real taster of being a martial arts instructor and, with Dave's help and support, I soon built up my confidence and embarked on another journey that was to change my life again, although not for several years to come. The one thing that I disagree with from my personal experience is students moving into the role of instructor too soon. I believe that in order to fully understand what you are teaching, you need to have lived it and, therefore, to have earned the right to teach it. Reality-based instructors talk about this all the time. How can you teach someone to survive on the streets when you haven't ever set foot outside yourself? At this point I felt I was learning the trade and had great fun doing it, but it wasn't until 11 June 2002 that I felt I was ready and confident enough to start my own school, a mere sixteen years after stepping into a martial art school for the first time.

Since that time I have continued my study of the martial arts, achieving my third dan in kickboxing on 21 June 2003 (I haven't got round to taking my fourth dan just yet, although it is now due) and gaining my latest black belt in January 2005 with the Keysi Fighting Method, a reality-based fighting system developed by Justo Dieguez and Andy Norman, two of the greatest martial artists I have had the honour of studying under. Martial arts have been a way of life for me now for over twenty years, and the values and life lessons I have learnt from my study have been invaluable. Ever since that fateful day trip to France that changed my life forever, I have been developing and growing my mental and physical ability. I would be lying if I said it had all been easy, as there have been many times when I have wanted to quit and far too many times to remember when I have had to step outside of my comfort zone (that invisible box that prevents us from growing or achieving our dreams). Despite all this, I wouldn't change anything I have done or achieved for the world – it's all character-building, so they say.

Achieving my black belt gave me a new-found belief that I could achieve anything I wanted in my life (and this book is proof of that). The memories of the attack in France, combined with the excellent role models I have had through my martial arts instructors, have prevented me from quitting when the going got tough and instilled in me a quality not seen in many people in today's society – the ability to never give up, no matter how tough something gets. As a result of my experiences in martial arts, kickboxing, flexibility training, dynamic kicking and tournament fighting, I hope you get as much out of reading this book as I did writing it.

Good luck in your training.

2 Warming Up

The warm-up is one of the most important aspects of any physical exercise, regardless of your chosen sport, hobby or activity. As such, great care and attention should be given to the warm-up stage to ensure that the risk of injury is minimized.

The role of the warm-up is quite simply to prepare the body for the physical work that is about to take place and it does this in the following ways:

- By raising the core-body temperature and in turn the heart rate for the start of the exercise.
- Warming up the muscles and loosening off the joints, allowing for greater all-round movement.
- Increasing oxygen utilization throughout the muscles, which is key in feeding the muscles with oxygenated blood during training, increasing blood flow throughout the body.
- Reducing muscle stiffness and thus eliminating, or reducing, the potential for muscle injury.

Think of a muscle like an elastic band. If you contract and relax the elastic band while cold, the movement will be a lot more resistant and will probably result in the band breaking under extreme pressure. However, if you warm the band up first and then place it under the same amount of stress, it is likely to stretch further and the potential for it to break is considerably reduced.

Warm-Up Drills

Most experienced martial artists will have a particular warm-up routine, which they follow prior to their specific training programme, and you will probably find that once you have a routine that suits you, you will stick to it for many years. However, many people don't actually understand how to warm the body up correctly and, in most cases, warm up with as much energy and vigour as the actual exercise they are about to undergo. The key rule with a good warm-up is to start off very gently and build up slowly. You also need to gear the warm-up to the same pace as the training that you are about to do. For example, if you are about to train ten rounds of heavy bag work, focusing predominately on kicking drills, then the warm-up will need to prepare the body to train at this pace. However, if you are just planning to work some light shadow sparring for a few rounds, then the warm-up doesn't need to be done to the same degree as it would for the bag workout example.

There are literally thousands of possible warm-up drills and routines you can follow, and to attempt to list them all would take up the whole of this book and probably leave you no time for your training. So, for now, the following warm-up exercises are an ideal starting point for the less experienced student and will set you up for the training you are about to do.

Warm-Up Routines

It will help if you have a timer (a digital kitchen countdown timer is ideal) or a large clock with a moving second hand for this part of your training. Be aware that the targets stated in this chapter are to be used as a guideline only and you may find it necessary to increase or reduce the suggested amount, based on your current level of fitness.

Get the Blood Pumping
Start off by bouncing from foot to foot on the balls of your feet for around thirty seconds. Be sure to keep your heels off the floor, as this will keep you light and agile, which is, of course, a trait that you need in kickboxing. Breathe in deeply through your nose and out through your mouth to fill the whole body with oxygen and help feed the muscles.

Continue breathing in this way for the whole of the warm-up routine.

Warm Up the Arms and Shoulders

Continue bouncing and, as you do, start rotating your wrists in a clockwise and anti-clockwise motion for a further thirty seconds – right hand, clockwise and left hand, anti-clockwise – for thirty seconds and then reverse the rotation on each hand for thirty seconds. Follow this by circling the lower arms from the elbow joint, in the same way as you did for the wrists, for a further thirty seconds, and finally circle both arms from the shoulder joint forwards for thirty seconds, backwards for thirty seconds and across the body for thirty seconds.

Warm Up the Lower Body

Now start jogging on the spot and, as you do, flick your heels up behind you as high as you can. Ideally you are looking to touch your body with the heels each time you bring them up. Continue at a relaxed pace for about a minute.

Continue jogging and, this time, bring the knees up so that they are at least level with your waist. Feel free to hold your hands out at waist height and touch each knee to the appropriate hand each time it comes up. Continue at a relaxed pace for about a minute.

Skipping

From here you can introduce some skipping into your warm-up. Skipping is a great cardio exercise and also helps with agility and timing. However, it does take a little practice if you've never skipped before. Ideally, forget how you used to skip when you were at school and try skipping like the boxers do. You can skip one-footed, on both feet or alternating between feet, but whichever way you choose, you just want to jump high enough for the rope to pass under you. Spin the rope using your wrists, as opposed to your arms, and stay light on your feet. To start with try skipping for a few minutes while you get used to it and as you get better, try increasing the length of time you skip in durations of one minute. You will also notice that as you improve you won't get as tired, so you will need to increase your intensity as well as your time in order to feel the benefits that this incredible exercise brings.

General Mobility Exercises

By now, you should be feeling slightly warmer and have loosened off the joints. As I previously mentioned, there are many things you can do to warm the body up but if you follow the previous routines to begin with, this will be a great start. Now we're going to loosen off the mid-section using some trunk twists and side-bend exercises. If you have a broom handle or something similar for this next part, you will find it advantageous. If not, then I will explain how to do the exercise without a broom handle.

Take your broom handle and rest it across the shoulders behind the neck. Now, instead of holding on to the ends of the broom handle as you would expect, roll your arms over the top so that your inner forearms rest on the handle and your arms hang down loosely. Stand with your feet just past shoulder-width apart and, with slightly bent knees, look straight ahead while you twist in a slow, deliberate movement from side to side. Repeat each twist twenty times off each side and then move on to the next exercise. Be sure to breathe out as you twist and in as you return to your start position.

If you don't have access to a broom handle, then simply interlock your fingers in front of your chest so that your arms are parallel to the floor and work the exercise this way instead.

Next, take hold of the broom handle at each end and, with slow, deliberate movements, bend as far to the side as you can. A good measure for this is to try and touch your elbow to your body each time you bend. Again aim for twenty per side, breathing out as you bend to the side and breathing in as you return to your start position.

If you don't have access to a broom handle, then simply rest your hands on your hips and slide your hand down the side of your body as you bend.

Warm-Up and Conditioning Exercises

This is the start of your basic warm-up routine and by now you should have started to loosen off the joints, warm the muscles up and raise the heart beat. A good test for this is to check your breathing.

If you are breathing just slightly heavier than you would at rest, then you have been successful with this part of your warm-up. If not, then next time try increasing the intensity of each exercise slightly so you can achieve that correct state. If you are breathing very heavily at this point, however, then you need to relax a little more and reduce some of the timings the next time you do this series of exercises.

Now move on to the following exercises, which will not only complete the warm-up but help to condition the body at the same time. Once you complete one exercise, move straight on to the next one.

The Star Jump – Jumping Jacks

As a complete beginner, aim for around ten star jumps to begin with and then, as your fitness develops, you can increase this number in multiples of five. Figure 1 shows the start point for the star jump and Figure 2 shows the finish point. The star jump will give you a total body workout.

The Push-Up

As a complete beginner, try aiming for around ten push-ups to start with and, as with the star jump, increase the number gradually as your fitness improves. Due to the nature of the push-up, you may find you are only able to increase the number by just one or two repetitions; this is completely normal, as your resistance for this exercise is of course your body weight. Unlike weight-training, where the weight can be increased or decreased in very small increments to allow for more repetitions, when your body is the weight, this is impossible.

There are many variations of push-up and the perfect push-up is a big debate among many sports people. However, to start with, try working the standard push-up that you will probably be more familiar with: Figure 3 shows the start point for the push-up; Figure 4 shows the finish point. Be sure to work the full push-up by bringing your body low to the ground and avoid the common 'cheat' characterized by only performing a half push-up, i.e.

Fig 1 Stand with your legs shoulder-width apart and hands by your side.

Fig 2 Jump in the air, opening your legs wider and bringing your arms out to form a star.

bringing the body only half-way down before pushing back up again. Figure 5 shows the muscles used when working the push-up.

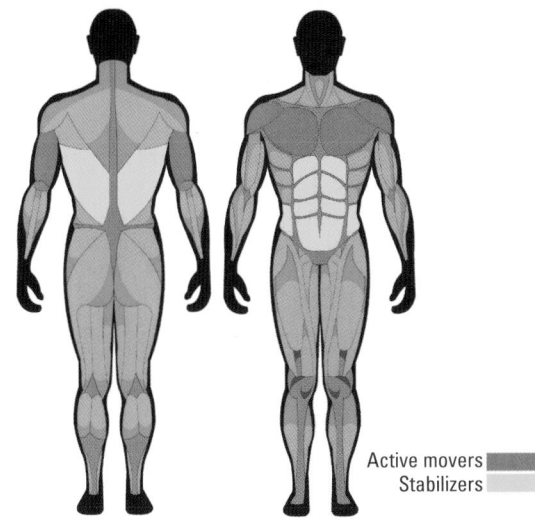

Fig 3 (top) Balance on the ball of one foot and place your arms out level with your shoulders at roughly double the width, keeping your body straight.

Fig 4 (above) Slowly lower your chest to the floor, inhaling and looking down as you do, and push back to the start position exhaling and keeping your body rigid.

Fig 5 (right) Muscles used for the push-up.

Active movers
Stabilizers

The Sit-Up

As with the push-up there is more than one way to perform a sit-up. The key with this exercise is to isolate the abdominal muscles and not the hips, and only use those muscles to move the body: Figure 6 shows the start point of a sit-up that isolates the abdominal muscles; Figure 7 shows the finishing point. Aim for ten sit-ups and increase the number gradually as your fitness improves. Be sure to work the correct technique for this exercise and avoid the common 'cheat' of swinging the arms towards the feet to assist with the upward movement or worse, holding on to the legs to make it easier. Figure 8 shows the muscles used when working the sit-up.

Fig 6 Keep your feet and shoulders off the floor and place your fingers on your temples.

Fig 7 Bring the elbows and the knees together, exhaling as you contract your body and inhaling on your return to the start point.

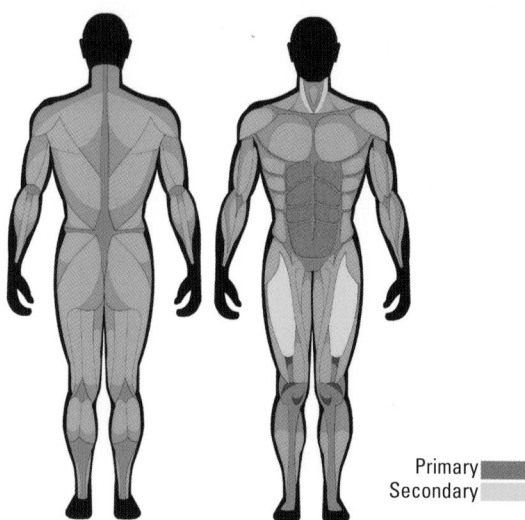

Primary
Secondary

Fig 8 Muscles used for the sit-up.

The Tuck Jump

This particular exercise is great for all-round conditioning but, in its full form, might be a little tough for the complete beginner: Figure 9 shows the start point for the tuck jump; Figure 10 shows the half-way point; Figure 11 shows the finish point. If you find this particular exercise a little tough, then miss out the half-way point (i.e. the bending of the legs) until your fitness improves. Aim for five to start with and increase the number gradually as your fitness improves. Figure 12 shows the muscles used when working the tuck jump.

Alternate Leg-Squat Thrust

Start off in a push-up style position but with your left knee touching your left elbow: Figure 13 shows the start point for this exercise. Change legs with a slight jumping motion and at the same time bring your head up towards the ceiling as you do: Figure 14 shows the finish point for this exercise. Each time your left knee touches your left elbow, count one. When you reach ten, change to the next exercise. Increase this exercise gradually as your fitness improves. Figure 15 shows the muscles used when working this exercise.

Fig 10 Keeping the back as straight as possible, bend the legs so the elbows touch the knees and take a deep breath in.

Fig 9 From standing, place your fingers on your temples.

Fig 11 Jump from this squat position, bringing the knees up to the elbows and exhale as you do.

15

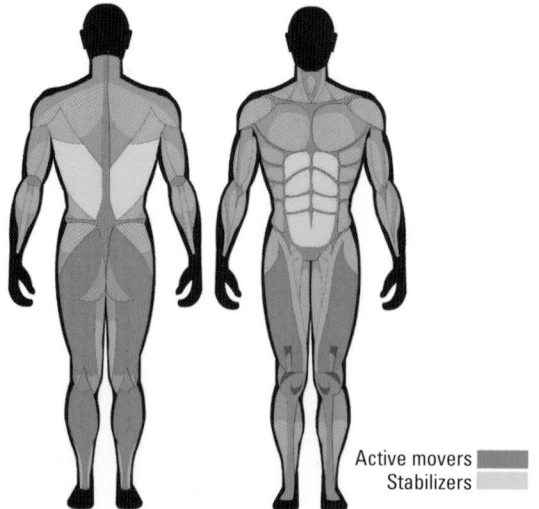

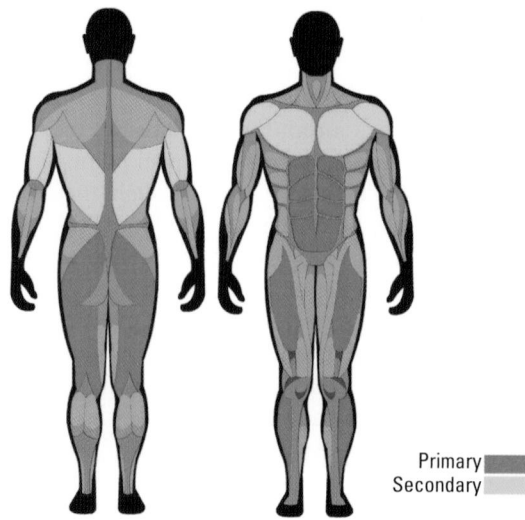

Active movers
Stabilizers

Primary
Secondary

The Burpee

This is the final exercise in this warm-up routine. It is probably the hardest of all the exercises so far but is definitely worth persevering with as it is the one that will fully challenge you and is one of the best complete body-conditioning exercises around: Figures 16 to 20 show the full range of movement required in order to perform the full burpee correctly. If you find this exercise tough to start with, miss out the middle stage and, instead, from the upright position simply bend forwards as if touching your toes and then straighten back up and jump in the air in one movement. This shortened version is known as a half-burpee. Try for five full-burpees or ten half-burpees as a starting point and, as with all the exercises covered so far, increase the number of repetitions you do as your fitness improves. Figure 21 shows the muscles used when working this exercise.

Fig 12 (top left) Muscles used for the tuck jump.

Fig 13 (middle left) The start point for the alternate leg squat thrust.

Fig 14 (bottom left) Rapidly change legs, keeping your upper body still and bringing your head up with each change.

Fig 15 (top right) Muscles used for the alternate leg squat thrust.

Fig 16 Start off in an upright position.

Fig 17 Bend the knees, bringing the hands to the floor.

Fig 18 Kick the legs back, as if performing a full squat thrust, and extend the body.

Fig 19 Bring the legs back in again.

Fig 20 From the squat position, jump up as high as you can in a similar motion to the star jump.

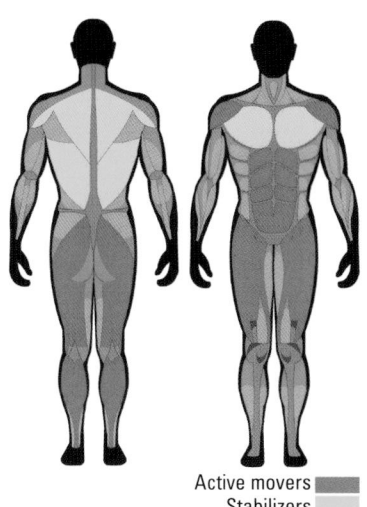

Active movers
Stabilizers

Fig 21 Muscles used for the burpee.

3 Stretching Techniques

As with a good warm-up routine prior to exercise, stretching also forms an essential part of any martial art, sport or physical activity, and never has stretching and flexibility training been more important than for the kickboxer. Having good upper-body movement is definitely essential in the world of martial arts; however, due to the huge part that kicking plays in kickboxing, and other arts that include kicking in their programme, flexibility of the lower body is of the utmost importance.

In order to become a successful kicker you need to build and develop muscles in the leg that are rarely used in everyday activities. These muscles and the tendons that surround them then need to be lengthened and stretched in order to increase their overall flexibility and movement. This in turn will improve the range of motion of the joints, allowing for greater overall ability and speed of movement all round. Even the most skilled kicker will require a good warm-up and stretching routine that they adhere to prior to their workout, and anyone that fails to warm up and stretch properly, runs the risk of straining and tearing muscles and ligaments that could result in long-term or even permanent damage.

There have been many books and articles written on the subject of stretching and flexibility, and attitudes towards the way we stretch today have changed over the years. At one time it was considered good practice to bounce when you performed leg-stretching exercises (ballistic stretching), as this helped the tendons to elongate at a much faster pace. However, after much research and investigation on the subject, this is now considered to be a dangerous way to stretch and can result in some serious, if not permanent, damage.

Stretching Methods

There are many ways with which to increase flexibility in the joints and some of these are listed below.

Static Stretching

This is probably the easiest and most common form of stretching and can be done as often as you like and anywhere you can fit it in. The basis of static stretching is to hold the position for between ten and thirty seconds, and to allow the muscles to relax into the stretch for the best results. The relaxation of the muscle helps to elongate it, which, if done over a period of time, helps to increase the overall length of the muscle, tendons and ligaments that surround it.

Passive Stretching

This is similar in motion to static stretching, however, you now use an external force to assist with the stretch. This can be in the form of weights, gravity, your own body, a partner or stretching machines and devices. Passive stretching has both its advantages and disadvantages, in as much as exerting force on to a limb will certainly increase the range of flexibility in a shorter time-frame; however, this type of attitude towards stretching greatly increases the risk of injury if care is not taken.

Active Stretching

This is the process of holding a limb in a set position for a period of time in order to facilitate a stretch. For example, extending a side kick as high as you can and holding it in this position using only the strength of the muscles that are being used to keep it in place. In order to be effective, this position needs to be maintained for a period of between ten and thirty seconds.

Ballistic Stretching

This type of stretching involves the bouncing technique previously mentioned and forces the limbs into an extended range of motion, whether the muscle is ready for it or not. There is a high probability of injury related to this form of stretching and, although it is the belief of some that ballistic stretching can increase flexibility at a quicker pace, it is certainly not recommended for the beginner or novice.

Dynamic Stretching

This is not dissimilar in principle to ballistic stretching but is considered a much safer alternative. Dynamic stretching involves the limb being propelled into its extended range of motion but not surpassing the natural overall movement of the limb. For example, performing a front rising kick, working up to full speed in the full range of motion: Figure 22 shows an example of a front rising kick being used for dynamic stretching. Dynamic stretches are useful in developing the neuro-muscular coordination for many of the kicks used in kickboxing, as well as developing speed and power.

Fig 22 Dynamic stretching using a front rising kick.

Isometric Stretching

Also know as PNF (proprioceptive neuromuscular facilitation), it is considered by most experts as the more effective and most comfortable form of stretching to develop flexibility. This method of stretching involves three key stages. Firstly, by using passive stretching, the muscle is stretched by an external force, such as a training partner or your own body weight. Secondly, when the stretch reaches its maximum limit, the muscle is then contracted as much as possible for a period of between ten and thirty seconds. Finally, the muscle is relaxed again and, as it is now tired as a result of the previous contraction, should relax even further allowing for a much greater stretch. This technique can then be repeated several times in succession enabling you to take full advantage of the results that this method of stretching offers. It should not, however, be performed on a daily basis as the muscles will need time to rest and repair, prior to their next isometric stretch.

The following are a series of safe and successful static and passive stretching drills that will help you to develop that much-needed level of flexibility without the risk of injury or damage. Be aware that everyone has varying levels of natural flexibility; therefore, a stretch that may be relatively easy for one person to perform may well be quite difficult for another. When you perform the following stretching exercises you should be able to 'feel' the stretch and this in turn will help you to understand which particular muscles, ligaments and tendons are currently being stretched. Be very careful, however, not to feel pain of any kind. It is quite normal, when stretching, to feel a warming sensation around the area being stretched, and this feeling is quite natural, especially if you consider that you are trying to manipulate your body into positions it is not used to being in. The term 'no pain, no gain' certainly *does not* apply to stretching. If you do feel pain of any kind, then you need to either relax a little so the pain stops, or stop completely to prevent the risk of damage or injury. Think of the elastic band once again. Although it is fully warmed up now, if you stretch it too far or too vigorously, it *will* still snap.

Fig 23 From an upright position ...

Stretching Routines

Be sure you are fully warmed up before attempting the following exercises.

From a standing position (Figure 23), bend from your waist, keeping the legs straight and try to touch your toes (Figure 24). If you can't yet touch your toes, then this is your goal for the next few months. If you can, then try to place your hands flat on the floor (Figure 25), and if you can achieve this, then try placing the back of your hands on the floor (Figure 26). Hold this stretch at your maximum position for a count of between ten and thirty seconds and then move on to the next exercise.

You may need to stand up and shake your legs out slightly after this last exercise and if so, this is completely normal when you first start stretching. Over time you will be able to move straight on to the next exercise but, as a beginner to static stretching, just go gently and listen to your body. This time go back to the last stretching exercise you did and now reach down and take hold of the back of your ankles (or as far down the legs as you can) and use this grip to gently pull your body down towards your legs (Figure 27). Again, hold this stretch for between ten and thirty seconds before moving on to the next exercise.

Fig 24 ... touch the toes.

Fig 25 Touch the floor.

Fig 26 Back of the hands on the floor.

Fig 27 Pull your body down.

Now sit on the floor and place your left leg out straight in front of you. Tuck your right leg into your body and grab hold of your foot, as shown. Support your left knee with your right hand to prevent it from bending or rising off the floor and gently lift your heel off the ground (Figure 28). Hold this stretch for between ten and thirty seconds. Now reach down your left leg with both hands and, at your lowest point, grab hold of your leg and gently pull yourself down, aiming to bring your chest as close as possible to your left leg (Figure 29). Hold this stretch for between ten and thirty seconds. Be sure to look at your leg as you hold the position and don't be tempted to look at your foot, as this puts unnecessary pressure on the neck and spine. Repeat on the other side.

Now place both legs out in front of you and, taking hold of both feet if you can, gently lift the heels off the floor (Figure 30). Hold this stretch for a count of between ten and thirty seconds. If you can't yet reach your feet, then simply lean forwards as if trying to touch your toes, for a count of between ten and thirty seconds, and then move on to the next part of this stretch. From here, either grab hold of your legs at your lowest point or slide the backs of your hands underneath your legs, as shown. Then gently pull your body down,

Fig 28 From a seated position, support your knee and lift your heel off the ground.

Fig 29 Reach down your leg and pull your body down.

Fig 30 Lift both heels off the floor.

Fig 31 Pull your body down to both legs.

aiming to get your chest as close to your legs as possible (Figure 31). Hold this stretch for between ten and thirty seconds.

From here we move into the hurdling stretch. This time curl your right leg around the rear of your body and keep your left leg out in front. Reach as far down your left leg as you can. Taking hold of your leg at its lowest point, gently pull your body down, as shown (Figure 32). Hold the position for between ten and thirty seconds, then walk your body around to your rear leg and pull yourself down as low as you can towards your right knee (Figure 33). Hold the position for between ten and thirty seconds. Repeat on the other side.

Fig 32 In a hurdling position, pull yourself down to your front leg.

Fig 33 Pull yourself down to your rear leg.

Fig 34 The butterfly stretch. Pull your feet into the body and push the knees to the floor using your elbows.

Fig 35 Place your left leg out straight, foot on the heel, and bend your right leg, foot on the ball.

This time we move into the butterfly stretch. In a seated position, with your legs bent (as shown), pull your feet in as close as you can to your body. Maintain a good grip on the feet with your hands and, using your elbows, gently push your legs down, attempting to get your knees as close to the floor as possible (Figure 34). Hold the position for between ten and thirty seconds.

From here we move on to the development of the splits. These are the stretches that most martial artists strive to attain and the ones that will greatly assist with the development of your flexibility for achieving that ultimate kick.

Place your left leg out to the side, so that your left foot rests on its heel with the toes pulled back towards the ceiling. Bend your right knee and ensure your body weight for this leg rests on the ball of your right foot. Take your right elbow inside the right knee and place your hands on the floor, as shown (Figure 35). To increase the intensity of this stretch, slide your left leg out towards the side and push your right knee out with your right elbow. Hold the position for between ten and thirty seconds and repeat on the other side.

This time adopt a similar position to the previous stretch, only now keep both feet flat on the floor, as shown (Figure 36). This will stretch the legs, muscles and tendons in a slightly different way and loosen up the joints in preparation for the box-split stretches. Hold the position for between ten and thirty seconds and repeat on the other side.

Now, from a standing position, open the legs to approximately double the width of your shoulders and, leaning forwards, take hold of both ankles.

Fig 36 Place your left leg out straight and bend your right leg, keeping both feet flat on the floor.

Fig 37 Open your legs approximately double shoulder-width and bring your body down to the centre.

Fig 38 Stretch over to your left leg.

Use this grip to pull your body down to the centre (Figure 37). Hold the position for between ten and thirty seconds. Ultimately, with this stretch you are aiming to pull your body through the centre of your legs for as far as you can and look up at the ceiling. Admittedly, this may take you a little while to achieve but it is possible with regular stretching.

From the previous stretch, lean over to your left leg and, if possible, take hold of your left foot with your right hand. Place your left hand on the back of your leg for support and pull the body down to your leg, as shown (Figure 38). If you are unable to reach your foot at this stage, then simply take hold of your leg at its lowest point and pull yourself down this way instead. Hold the stretch for between ten and thirty seconds and repeat on the other side.

Now, supporting yourself with your hands, keep your feet flat on the floor and slide your legs out as wide as they will go (Figure 39). From this position, keep your feet where they are and walk yourself backwards so that your hands end up under your body and your feet now face the ceiling (Figure 40). From here, bring your chest down as low as you can towards the floor as if you are about to do a close-grip push-up. Your feet should now be on their sides (Figure 41) (notice the difference in your foot position compared to Figure 39). Push yourself backwards so that you

once again come up on to your heels, with your body weight resting on your hands (Figure 42). Repeat this forwards and backwards movement for a further three or four times holding the final position (i.e. Figure 37) for around ten seconds each time, before repeating the whole sequence again.

Fig 39 Slide the legs wide apart, taking your body weight on your hands.

Fig 40 Walk backwards and place your hands underneath your body, bring your feet on to their heels.

Fig 41 Bring the chest to the floor, supporting yourself with your hands.

From the last exercise, sit down on the floor keeping the legs as wide as you can and place your hands in the centre (Figure 43). Make sure you are at your widest point by shuffling into your maximum stretching position. If you place a hand behind your body and one in front, you will find that you can lift yourself up and slide yourself forward, which will help you find that maximum position.

NB At this early stage in your flexibility training you may well find your legs do not open as wide as shown in the photographs. This is completely normal and will improve over time and with regular training, so persevere and remember that stretching is all about little and often, in other words little improvements on a regular basis, as opposed to huge improvements every now and again.

Fig 42 Push backwards and hold the position for ten seconds.

Fig 43 Open your legs as wide as you can. You may need to shuffle forwards to find your maximum position.

Fig 44 (top) Bring your elbows and forearms to the floor.

Fig 45 (bottom) Bring your chest down to the floor and hold the position.

From here, try and place your elbows and forearms flat on to the floor (Figure 44). Relax into the stretch and hold it for between ten and thirty seconds. You now need to bring your chest down as close as you can to the floor and hold the position once more for between ten and thirty seconds (Figure 45).

NB Remember you should be able to feel these stretches but they shouldn't hurt. If you do experience any kind of pain, then reduce the intensity or stop altogether. You may also find that with this last stretch, and particularly with the following one, because they need to be held in position for a certain length of time, a cramp-like sensation may well set in. If this is the case, then simply stop the stretch, have a walk around and try again once the sensation subsides.

For the final set of stretching exercises, we are now going to focus on the front-split stretch. From a forwards-facing position, keep your right leg straight and bend your left leg (Figure 46). Try not to lean forwards with this stretch and it may also help if you rest your hands on the legs, as shown. Hold the stretch for between ten and thirty seconds.

From here, straighten the left leg and gently lean down, attempting to bring your chest as close to the straight leg as possible (Figure 47). You may also find with this stretch that taking hold of your leg and pulling down slightly with your hands may help bring your chest down further. Hold this position for between ten and thirty seconds. Finally, support your body weight with your hands and gradually slide the rear leg back, bringing your body into a front-split stretch (Figure 48). Hold the position for between ten and thirty seconds before lowering the body down towards the outstretched leg (Figure 49).

This complete warm-up and stretching programme should take you somewhere between twenty and forty minutes, depending on the length of time you rest between sets and how familiar you are with the exercises described. There is no real rule to how long a warming-up and stretching session should take. The length of time you intend to train for, and the type of training you are about to undergo, will probably influence the length of time this stage takes. If you only intend to train lightly for thirty minutes,

Fig 46 Developing the front split stretch.

Fig 47 Straighten the lead leg and bring the body down.

Fig 48 (top) Taking the body weight on the hands, slide the rear leg back into the splits.

Fig 49 (bottom) Bring the head down to the outstretched leg to complete the stretch.

a twenty-minute warm-up may be too much. But if you intend to train for several hours at maximum intensity, it may be too little.

Be aware that every experienced martial artist will have their own favourite warm-up and stretching routines, and once you become confident and more experienced with the workouts, you may also want to develop your own. As a beginner to kickboxing, the warm-up and stretching drills described in this section will serve you well and will ensure that you can move on to the next stage of your training, secure in the knowledge that you have warmed yourself up and stretched yourself out, correctly.

4 Stances and Footwork

Before we start to look at the punching and kicking side of kickboxing, it's important to understand how we stand and how we move. Getting this right early on will make a big difference to your overall ability and will help to build strong foundations that will carry you through your many years of training. Think of it like building a house. If the foundations are strong, the house will last forever and weather almost any storm. If the foundations are weak, the house, although appearing strong at first glance, may well crumble with the first gust of wind. Because of this, developing your basic foundation is more important than any other part of your training, and neglecting this simple rule could have dire consequences later on.

The Stances

A good stance is of major importance to the kickboxer because this will not only help with attack and defence ability, but also with weight distribution, balance and movement. If your stance is poor, then one of these attributes may well be missing and a good attack from an opponent may well finish the fight. If your stance is good, however, it will help you to absorb an attack better, as well as move faster, counter quicker and deliver knock-out power.

There is certainly more than one way to stand and you may well develop a preferred stance over time; however, in order to remain as versatile as you can while you move from kicks, to punches, to evasions, to counters and so on, you will need to remain flexible in your position and may well switch from one stance to another and back again during a fight.

The Basic Stances

Get a feel for the stances below by working them in front of a mirror, if you can. Pay particular attention to any gaps you may leave in your defence, which will be a natural target for your opponent, and see how the particular stance feels overall. Transition between stances to see how it feels and try to incorporate them with the footwork drills described later. The general rule regarding stances in kickboxing is that you lead with your weakest side and your strongest side is generally the one you put to the rear. For example, if you are right-handed (the hand you would normally write with) then your left side needs to go in front and your right side goes back.

The Front Stance
This is a more popular stance when predominantly using your hands or front-facing kicks. The feet are positioned around shoulder width apart with the weight evenly distributed between both legs. The front and rear legs are evenly spaced and the rear foot is resting on the ball. The lead hand is slightly in front of the face with the lead shoulder raised up to protect the chin. The rear hand is resting on the other side of the chin and the elbows are tucked in tight to the body. Finally, shrug your shoulders to add further protection to the neck and prevent the whiplash effect that can occur when receiving head shots. Figure 50 shows the stance from a front on view and Figure 51 shows the stance from a side-on view. This stance is ideal for close-range fighting when punching is paramount; however, against a good kicker in the kicking range, it can have a few weaknesses.

The Angled Stance
This stance is generally ideal for working more of the angular attacks, such as the round kicks, axe kicks, spinning kicks, and still allows access to the major punches and hand techniques. The other benefit it has is that it limits the target area available

Fig 50 The front stance – front-on.

Fig 51 The front stance – side-on.

Fig 52 The angled stance – front-on.

Fig 53 The angled stance – side-on.

to your opponent and is ideal for mid- to long-range fighting. This time there is a shorter distance between the feet compared to the front stance (the feet are almost on the same line), with the rear leg positioned almost directly underneath the body. The weight distribution is now around 70 per cent on the rear leg and 30 per cent on the front leg. The body is turned slightly to one side but not completely side on, showing more of the lead shoulder than the rear. The lead hand now comes down, offering a different kind of protection to the body, and the chin tucks away behind the lead shoulder. The rear hand moves slightly further forwards to protect the other side of the face and the elbows remain tucked in tight against the body (Figures 52 and 53). This stance has the flexibility of long-range fighting with the added advantage of hand availability for close range. It can offer slightly more protection against a good kicker, providing the chin is kept well protected with the lead shoulder, and it also allows for explosive attacking with the kicks due to the weight distribution.

The Side Stance

As the name suggests, this stance involves the body being completely side-on. It is a stance favoured a lot by the freestyle fighters because it offers very little target area to the opponent and allows for a very fast, explosive technique, in particular the back fist and the side kick. On its own it can limit a lot of rear-attacking techniques, such as a cross-punch or rear-leg static kick due to the rear hand and leg becoming blocked by the front side. However, it is an excellent stance to work the majority of spinning attacks from. The feet are now on the same straight line and the body is turned completely side-on. The chin tucks away behind the lead shoulder and the lead arm is positioned down and across the front of the body to add protection to this area. The rear hand can be positioned on the other side of the chin, as before, or in front of the chin resting on the lead shoulder and the elbows are tucked in tight to the body. The weight distribution is around 70/30 per cent, as before, and the rear leg sits directly underneath the body with the body leaning slightly back (Figures 54 and 55).

Fig 54 The side stance – front-on.

Fig 55 The side stance – side-on.

These three stances work in combination with one another and the key is to be able to move seamlessly from one to the other as quickly and as smoothly as possible. Regardless of which aspect of your training you are working on, bag work, sparring, focus pads and so on, you need to develop the ability to transition between the stances based on your position, your intended technique, the energy you are giving, as well as the energy you are receiving, and all the other major factors that determine how you move, instead of simply limiting yourself to one stance and one stance only. You also need to understand that you have to stay relaxed as you move. Tensing up and staying fixed in your position will limit your ability, as well as add resistance to your movement, which in turn will slow you down. The stances described above are there to help you understand how to stand correctly. The reality is that you need to use each in a realistic way while you train and develop them in such a way that they work comfortably for you.

Footwork

Footwork is the particular part of the training that helps us to move around in our stance, and this section is crucial in helping to build strong foundations. There are eight major footwork steps that can be used in kickboxing and the one that you choose to use can be governed by factors such as your intended attacking (or defending) technique, distance (in relation to the target/opponent), energy (how much you intend to give to your technique) and position (either your position or that of your target/opponent). In the following section we will look at the various steps that can be used and work these steps in isolation in order to understand exactly how they work before adding them to the rest of the drills.

The Various Footwork Steps

Try working the following footwork steps, in various ways, to get a feel for how they can be used in as many different scenarios as possible. Here are some training drills to help you get started.

Allowing two to three minutes for each step:

• Isolate each step in turn and practise it with each stance. This will help you to understand which stance complements which footwork drill.

• Isolate each step in turn and practise it with each technique. This will help you to understand which technique works better with which type of footwork.

• Isolate each step and each technique and introduce training aids such as a heavy bag, Thai pads, focus pads. This will give you a feel for which footwork drill is most effective for getting the best out of each technique.

Work with a sparring partner, either with contact or non-contact, based on how you feel at this stage (*see* Chapter 11 for more information on sparring). This will ultimately tell you how each step works when faced with a realistically moving target.

The Simple Step Forwards

This is used predominantly for covering distance and adding energy when punching. The simple step involves pushing off with the ball of your rear foot, enabling you to step forwards quickly with your lead leg, and then dragging the rear foot up behind to re-stabilize you and bring you back into your stance. Try this one while standing in a front stance to begin with (Figures 56 and 57).

Fig 56 The initial step, pushing off with the rear foot.

The Simple Step Backwards

In exactly the same way as the simple step forwards, the same step works equally as well backwards, only this time reversing the movement. Push off the ball of your lead foot and step backwards with your rear leg, dragging the front leg back to bring you into your stance once again (Figures 58 and 59).

The Simple Step with Zone

This is a slight variation on the last step due to the fact that you now step slightly to one side (either left or right with your lead or rear leg, depending on which leg you have in front). To help you understand how this might be used, think of how you might step to the side slightly to avoid a straight punch from an opponent. Zoning out helps to utilize footwork within an attack and keeps the head off the centre line. For example, in a left lead, you may use a simple step forwards to set up a jab to the head and then step to the side (i.e. zone out to the left) to set up the cross-punch off the rear hand or perhaps a body-hook off the lead hand (Figures 60 and 61).

Fig 58 Push backwards with the ball of the lead foot.

Fig 57 The rear leg drags to reset the stance.

Fig 59 Drag the lead leg back into line.

Fig 60 Simple step and zone to the left.

Fig 61 The rear leg drags to reset the stance.

Fig 62 Push off and step up to the front leg with the rear leg.

Fig 63 Using the energy of the initial step, skip forward with the front leg.

The Shuffle Step Forwards

This is used for covering slightly longer distance, particularly when kicking. Push off using the ball of the rear foot and step up to the front foot (not past it) with the rear foot. Then, using a skipping-like motion, step forward with the front leg (Figures 62 and 63). This step is generally used for shorter range kicking, when you are just out of punching range but could kick with little to no real movement. You will find that this step will certainly help to add energy to the kick, whether movement was necessary or not.

The Shuffle Step Backwards

As with the shuffle step forwards, the same movement can be used to move backwards. Transfer your weight to your back leg and bring the lead leg up to the rear leg using a skipping-style movement and step back with your rear leg to reset your stance (Figures 64 and 65). This movement can be used to quickly avoid a forward attack from an opponent.

The Slide Step

Not quite as quick as the shuffle step, however, due to the nature of the movement, this step has the potential to project you over a greater distance. As with the shuffle step, it can be used in conjunction with most of the basic techniques and works particularly well with the angled stance or side stance. Slide the rear foot up to the lead foot and then slide the front foot forwards to cover distance. If done using a slight skipping motion, this technique can be used to generate a noticeable increase in power when used in conjunction with a kick (Figures 66 and 67).

The Slide Step Backwards

Once again, this simple step can also be used to move backwards. The benefit you may have with this is that it will move you further out of range of an attack. Slide the front foot backwards until it meets the rear foot and then slide the rear foot back into your stance (Figures 68 and 69).

Fig 64 Using a skipping motion, bring your lead leg back to your rear leg.

Fig 65 Step back with your rear leg to reset your stance.

Fig 66 Slide your back foot up to your lead foot.

Fig 67 Slide the lead foot forwards to reset your stance.

Fig 68 Slide the lead foot up to the back foot.

Fig 69 With a skipping motion, slide the rear foot back into your stance.

The Cross-Step Forwards

This is a step that can be used to cover an even greater distance than the previous two steps (the shuffle step and the slide step) and, if used correctly, can deliver the maximum power you may get from a static kick. The only real downside to this type of movement is that it works better at a distance and so can be fairly easy to counter or avoid. Step either behind or in front of the lead foot with the rear foot, and then complete the movement by stepping forward with the lead foot. The further you step with the rear foot, the greater the distance you can cover with this movement (Figures 70 and 71). The technique that you are going to use with this step will greatly determine whether you step in front or behind the lead foot. A side kick, for example, works better if you step behind; however, a round kick works better if you step in front.

The Cross-Step Backwards

An excellent defensive step, which can move you out of the way of an attack very quickly. With your lead foot, step backwards and past your rear foot, sliding your rear foot back into your stance (Figures 72 and 73).

The Full Step

This step works well with the majority of kicks, including rear-leg kicks, spinning kicks and jumping kicks. It can be used to cover distance and enhance the overall power of a kick, when used properly. Step through with the rear leg so that it becomes the front leg. The further forwards you step with this, the greater distance you will cover. Be aware that this is a step used to set up a kick, hence the position of the body after the movement (Figures 74 and 75). In the same way as the full step forwards, a simple reversal of the movement will project you backwards.

Fig 70 Step behind the lead foot with the rear foot.

Fig 71 Step forwards with the lead foot to reset the stance.

Fig 72 Step backwards with your lead leg crossing the path of your rear leg.

Fig 73 Bring the rear leg back into position.

Fig 74 In a front stance …

Fig 75 … step forwards with your rear leg in preparation for a kick.

The Switch Step

A favourite with the full-contact fighters due to the power that can be generated, the switch step is an on-the-spot change of stance used to generate a power kick to a particular target; for example, a power round-kick to the body, when both fighters have their left legs in front. This step will not necessarily cover much, if any, distance but, with practice, it can deliver a powerful rear-leg kick, where a front-leg kick would otherwise have been used (Figures 76 and 77).

The Spin Step

Of all the various steps covered here, the spin step is the one that you need to be most careful with, for the simple reason that you turn your back on your opponent. As anyone that has ever fought in competition or on the street will know, turning your back on an opponent can be a very unwise move, especially if your opponent has a great deal of skill and experience. For this reason, the spin step is a movement that you need to be completely competent with before using it in a realistic situation. Spin backwards 180 degrees, bringing your rear foot to the front. For the best description of this movement, we'll work from a left lead in a side stance (left leg in front and side on). Spin 180 degrees clockwise landing with your right foot in front. If done correctly this will have the effect of projecting you forwards at the same time (Figures 78 and 79).

The Hop-Step

For a kicker, the hop-step is possibly the greatest movement of all. If done correctly, this step has the potential to cover distance without telegraphing (pre-movement that gives away your intent to attack) the technique that you are about to use. Giving away what you are about to do by telegraphing is a common mistake that most inexperienced fighters make and this movement is a great way to reduce the risk of making any pre-kick movements. Due to the complexity of it, however, it is also one of the most difficult to master. To help you understand this movement, we're going to over-exaggerate the technique until you become comfortable with it. Begin the step by slightly lifting the lead leg off the floor in readiness to kick (Figure 80).

Fig 76 Jump and switch the legs as quickly as you can.

Fig 77 Land back in your stance with the opposite leg now in front.

Fig 78 With your left leg in front, spin 180 degrees clockwise.

Fig 79 Bringing your rear leg to the front.

Fig 80 Bring the lead leg off the floor in readiness for the kick.

Fig 81 Hop towards your target, executing the kick at the same time.

In order to carry out this simple move, you first need to ensure that your stance isn't too wide. If you have to step up slightly with your rear leg to aid your balance, in order to lift the front foot off the floor, your stance is too long. Try starting the movement with your rear leg positioned directly underneath your body for support, thereby allowing you to raise the front leg without being off-balance and avoid telegraphing the movement. This may appear strange at first, however, with practice it will feel more natural. Once you become used to this step, the need to lift the lead foot off the floor will reduce and you will be able to execute the step with both feet on the floor. However, when first learning this footwork drill, the temptation is still to step if the stance is too long.

From here you simply hop towards your target while executing the kick at the same time (Figure 81). The kick and the hop should ideally land together. For now, however, just focus on the footwork and we'll add the kick in later.

This movement can be used effectively with all but the spinning kicks and is especially useful in conjunction with double kicks. Reverse the procedure to move backwards using the hop-step technique.

You should now have a basic understanding of how to stand, how to move and how to use your footwork to full advantage and to get the best out of your training. Remember, the majority of these footwork drills can be used from any stance and with any technique, and what works effectively with a forward attack, can work just as effectively with a movement backwards and counter-attack. What you now need to do is determine which combinations work best for you, and this you will only find out through practice and training.

5 Hand Techniques

There are just six basic punches in the art of kick-boxing, and if no other hand techniques had been introduced, these six punches are so effective that they have served the boxing world more than adequately since John Sholto Douglas, the 9th Marquis of Queensberry, introduced the modern-day rules for boxing back in 1867. These six basic punches can be used to attack at almost any range and angle, and when combined with a good understanding of stance, footwork, timing and movement, can be used with devastating effect. In this chapter we are going to look at these six basic punches in detail, as well as the many other hand techniques that help to make kickboxing the incredible art that it is.

Basic Punches

Jab, cross, lead-hook, rear-hook, lead-uppercut and rear-uppercut are the six basic punches that are found in all boxing-related arts, and the attitude towards these punches from each art is pretty much the same. Modern-day boxing, or Western boxing, as it is also referred to, is renowned for its tough and rigorous approach to training and fighting, and these same six punches are so effective that they have been adopted by many of the top sport fighting arts, such as boxing, right through to kickboxing and karate.

The advantage a kickboxer may have over a boxer is the ability to use certain other hand techniques not found in boxing. These additional hand techniques might include elbows, forearms, back fist strikes and spinning techniques and, depending on the kickboxing style that is studied, knifehand-style strikes as well. We will endeavour to look at all the main hand-related attacking techniques that a kickboxer could use in this chapter. Be aware, however, that there are many styles, arts and authorities out there that may all use the same techniques but in a slightly different way. Even individuals within the same fighting art may have changed or adapted a specific technique to make it more effective or unique to them. This doesn't necessarily make it wrong or ineffective, it just makes it work for that individual in a different way.

As you read through the next few chapters, understand that, in reality, a whole book could probably be written on each individual technique and the many different ways it could be used. What you have to do, is take the information you receive, train it and make it work for you.

The Jab

Probably one of the most used and important punches in the kickboxer's arsenal. The jab is a straight attacking fast punch that is thrown off the lead hand. It is not considered to be a knockout punch but instead is used to judge distance, probe through an opponent's defence and set up the more powerful knockout-style punch. It is also used for long-range punching and, therefore, has the furthest reach of all the basic punches.

The striking part of the jab is the front of the first two knuckles with the wrist kept straight and the thumb tucked underneath the fist (Figure 82). From a front stance, with the guard held high (Figure 83), extend the lead arm out in a straight line towards your target. Stay relaxed as the arm travels out and tense only at the point of impact (Figure 84). At full extension, bring the lead shoulder up to protect the chin and once used, bring the jab back into place to continue using it as part of your guard. To add additional energy and further protection to the jab, turn the body inwards slightly as the punch finds its mark.

Fig 82 Strike with the front of the first two knuckles.

Fig 83 In a front-on stance, facing your opponent.

Fig 84 Extend the lead hand straight out, striking with the knuckles.

The Cross

Used off the rear hand, the cross is probably one of the most powerful of all the hand techniques and a definite knockout punch, if used correctly. There is much debate as to the most effective part of the fist with which to strike, as some arts will favour the first two knuckles (the index and middle finger), whereas other styles favour the last three knuckles (the middle, ring and little finger). There is a higher risk of hand injury occurring when the little finger knuckle is used to strike with, particularly in the case of bare-knuckle punching or board breaking (a training method practised by the karate and tae kwon do arts). So, as a beginner to kickboxing, it is highly advisable to protect your hand with a good hand wrap and either bag gloves or boxing gloves before embarking on a heavy punching session.

Like the jab, the cross-punch is a straight technique that can be used very effectively from a distance. From your front stance in a left lead, zone out slightly to the left (Figure 85). This simple movement will move your head off the centre line, thereby making it a harder target to hit as you move in. It will also bring you closer to your opponent, allowing for more energy to be inserted into the punch at the point of impact. From here, snap the punch out towards the target in a straight line directly from the guard position (Figure 86). At the point of impact, the rear shoulder should be protecting the right side of the chin and the lead hand should be protecting the left side. You can also add further protection to the body by keeping your left arm in tight to act as a shield against a possible counter-kick or punch. Once the cross has been used, you can then either continue your attack, using additional punch or kick combinations, or use your footwork to move you back to a favourable stance and position.

The Lead-Hook

Hooking punches are designed for close-range fighting and are more commonly used once the straight punches have done the job of bringing you in nearer to your opponent. The punch is generally thrown in a semicircular motion, keeping the arm bent at roughly 90 degrees and targeting the side of the head or body. Due to the reaction of the head once a hooking punch lands, they are more commonly responsible for the knockout than the majority of the other punches when facing an opponent front-on. To add additional energy, the body can be turned in an arc, pivoting with the lead foot and driving the full force of the whole body behind the punch.

From your front stance in a left lead, zone to the left, bringing the hands in close to protect the chin and the elbows in tight to protect the body (Figure 87). Turn the body in, pivoting on the lead foot and as you do, allow the punch to travel directly from the chin to the target (Figure 88). Try to avoid swinging the punch out, which is the natural thing to do when you first start learning this technique, as this will open you up and make you more vulnerable to a counter-attack. The hand position at the point of impact can be either vertical (as shown) or horizontal, and this can be down to several factors, such as body position, distance and angle of attack.

Fig 85 Zone out to the left to set up the punch.

Fig 86 The cross lands.

Fig 87 Zone out to set up the punch.

Fig 88 The lead hook lands.

The Rear-Hook

This punch works in exactly the same way as the lead-punch, it just comes off the rear hand. Most rear-hand punches are generally considered to be more powerful than the lead-hand punches and so for that reason, the rear-hooking punch can be quite a devastating technique, if done properly. The only real downside with rear punches is that they have further to travel compared to the lead and, therefore, can sometimes be a little slower landing. When faced with an experienced opponent, this can be a disadvantage. Therefore, the lead-hand punches are generally used prior to engaging the rear hand in a bid to 'set up' the rear-hand attack.

From your front stance in a left lead, zone out to the right with your rear leg, keeping the hands around the chin area and the elbows into the body for protection (Figure 89). As you step, slightly adjust the position on your rear shoulder in readiness for the punch. You should now be in the ideal range for the rear-hooking punch to work. From here turn your whole body in an anti-clockwise motion towards your opponent, keeping your arm at a 90-degree angle, and strike the target using the full energy of the pivot and not just the power of the arm (Figure 90). Don't forget, as with all the punches, this works equally well to the body as it does to the head.

The Lead-Uppercut

The uppercut is a vertical, rising punch designed to attack the chin or the body from relatively close range. It can be done at a slight distance; however, the punch then changes form slightly and you may find that a jab or cross could be used more effectively when the distance is increased. As with all the punches so far, additional energy can be added to the uppercut by way of the body and leg movement.

Fig 89 Zone out to set up the punch.

Fig 90 The rear hook lands.

Fig 91 Zone out to set up the punch.

Fig 92 The lead uppercut lands.

From a front stance in a left lead, zone out slightly with your lead leg, keeping your guard tight to prevent a counter-attack (Figure 91). Adjust your lead shoulder in readiness for the punch and, keeping the fist on your chin until the very last minute, drive the punch upwards towards the target, powering through with your body and legs, and striking with the inner part of the fist facing towards you (Figure 92).

The Rear-Uppercut

The principle for the rear-uppercut is much the same as it is for the lead. You will probably find this punch more natural and it will certainly have greater power and energy. Once again, the rear-uppercut can be directed towards the body or the head and, depending on your position and angle, this could be either to the front or the side of the target.

From a front stance in a left lead, zone out slightly to the right to bring you closer to your target, at the same time as keeping your head off the centre line (Figure 93). Keep the guard tight to

prevent a counter-attack and adjust the rear shoulder in readiness for the punch. Power through with the whole body, driving the arm in a direct line to the target and keeping the fist turned in towards you as it makes the connection (Figure 94).

Advanced Techniques

The advanced techniques are the additional techniques that separate one art-form from another. In kickboxing, depending on the style studied (full-contact, semi-contact, freestyle and so on, there are many additional techniques, aside from the obvious kicking ones, that can be used, and this next section will help you to understand and clarify how they all work.

The Lead Elbow Strike

The elbow strike is one of the kickboxer's most vicious weapons and has the potential to end a fight very quickly. Generally found in the full-contact arena, it is a close-range attacking weapon that can travel in an ascending, descending, semicircular or

Fig 93 Zone out to set up the punch.

Fig 94 The rear uppercut lands.

even spinning motion, and can, therefore, be used from any angle or position. The striking part for this technique is the tip of the elbow and, due to the close distance you will find yourself in with this technique, the head needs to be covered as much as possible as the elbows are used.

From a front stance in a left lead, zone out slightly to the left to set up the elbow strike. As you start your attack, keep your striking hand in place at the side of your face and bring your rear arm up, placing your hand on your head to give you additional protection (Figure 95). If done properly, you will still be able to see your opponent through the gap you make with your rear arm. From the set-up position, twist your whole body in a semicircular motion towards the target, keeping the rear hand in place throughout, and raising the lead arm up to set the elbow up for the connection (Figure 96).

The Rear Elbow Strike
The rear elbow strike works in a similar way to the lead elbow with emphasis on the movement of the body and the protection of the head due to the close range you will find yourself in. The elbow strike is probably one of the few techniques that brings you in so close to your opponent, therefore, as effective as it is, it also needs to be used with careful consideration as to the effectiveness of your counter-defences.

This time we will look at an alternate way of using the elbow to give you a different perspective of how the set-up can also work. From your front stance in a left lead, bring your lead arm up and place your hand on your head, adding that much-needed cover to the technique. At the same time, raise the rear arm up level with your chin and parallel to the floor (Figure 97). This is your start position. Zone out slightly to the left to bring you in closer to your opponent and to keep your head off the centre line, and as you move, power through with your body turning into the technique in a semicircular, anti-clockwise motion and driving the elbow through to find its target (Figure 98).

Fig 95 Zone out to set up the lead elbow strike.

Fig 96 The lead elbow lands.

Fig 97 Set up for the rear elbow strike.

Fig 98 The rear elbow strike lands.

The Back Fist Strike

Apparently, this was one of Bruce Lee's favourite techniques. If done properly, this technique can be as fast as lighting. The back fist strike works along very similar lines to the jab, in as much as it is probably not going to deliver knockout power but instead is designed to stun your opponent, allowing for the delivery of a knockout technique. The back fist is mainly thrown off the lead hand, as this is a much faster way to use it. However, it can also be done with the rear hand but you may find this to be somewhat more awkward in comparison. The only exception to this rule is when you add a spin to the technique, as this changes the back fist strike into a potentially devastating knockout technique and is very simple to execute.

From your left lead, and working in a front stance, bring your lead hand in towards your chin so that your lead elbow points towards your opponent (Figure 99). Extend the lead arm out towards its target (Figure 100), connect and retract the arm as fast as you can, using a whipping-like motion. The striking part for this technique is the first two knuckles with the fist turned on its side, as shown. A mistake that many people make with the back fist strike is to hit and follow through. Although this can certainly add additional power to the technique, it does have a tendency to leave you slightly open and unguarded in the event of a counter-strike from your opponent.

The Spinning Back Fist Strike

This technique is one of very few spinning-hand techniques that you are likely to find in kickboxing (or many fighting arts for that matter) and is definitely a knockout one if done correctly. The energy generated from the spin can be quite considerable and if you add a jump in at the same time, the overall result can be quite devastating. The only disadvantage this technique has is that you do turn your back on your opponent, which is never a wise thing to do, especially if your opponent is quite experienced. However, if your timing is good and you have set the technique up correctly, as you only show your back for a split second, there is a very high chance this won't cause you any real problem.

Fig 99 Set up for the lead back fist strike.

Fig 100 The back fist strike lands.

From your front stance and working in a left lead (Figure 101), twist your body round in a clockwise motion, bringing your striking arm up to cover your face and to form a barrier adding additional protection from a counter-strike (Figure 102). Ensure you whip your head round as fast as you can to check the position and status of your opponent prior to executing the technique. Extend the striking arm out, connecting with the target in the same way as you would for a standard back fist strike (Figure 103). After the attack, you can either retract the arm and reset your stance, by stepping backwards with your left leg into a right lead, or you can hit and follow through with the technique stepping round with your right leg and through with your left leg bringing you closer in to your opponent and setting you up for a possible hand and/or leg combination attack at the same time. Just be careful to avoid spinning back again as this will involve you presenting your back for a second time and can be considered a risky manoeuvre, particularly if the spinning back fist doesn't do its job.

Fig 101 From a front stance position.

Fig 102 Guard the head and start the spin.

Fig 103 The spinning back fist lands.

Training Drills

Training drills are a vital part of the kickboxer's training regime, as without them, there is no way of improving a technique any further. Repetition of each technique through practice and training is crucial if you are to develop not only the technique, but the motor skills that are also involved in performing the full technique correctly. Muscle memory is a term often used within the sporting world and this is the body's ability to remember a specific action to a point where conscious thought can be removed. This then means that the ability to perform the movement, complete with the intricacies associated with that movement, become natural and almost automatic and can, therefore, be called upon at any time without the need to 'think' about each separate part of the associated movement.

Driving a car is a great example of how muscle memory works. When we first start out learning to drive there are a multitude of factors that have to be taken into account, just simply to get the car moving. Initially, each factor has to be constantly recalled and in every case this will be done with conscious thought. After several months of driving, however, it would be considered quite natural to simply 'jump' in the car and drive off. This doesn't mean the previous factors are no long necessary, it just means that through practice and repetition, the necessity to consciously think about each factor is no longer essential, as the body remembers exactly what it has to do (muscle memory) and, as a bonus to this, it can perform these exact same actions at a much faster rate.

The same is true in kickboxing. To the experienced kickboxer, a jab is simply a jab. To the beginner, however, the jab is made up of a series of individual movements incorporating footwork and correct body positioning, as well as a good understanding of hand positioning, energy, line of travel and defence. And this is on a target that isn't moving or trying to hit back. Therefore, you should aim to train each individual technique a minimum of two-thousand times before you can say you 'fully' understand how it works.

It is highly recommended that you are fully warmed up, have stretched correctly and wear hand wraps and a good-quality bag glove or boxing glove, as well as appropriate elbow protectors and training supports if needed, to prevent the risk of injury before commencing the following training drills.

Focus-Pad Training

With a training partner, holding a pair of focus pads as shown (Figures 104–109), isolate each of the techniques detailed in the last section and train them in the following ways:

- Pad holder remains stationary throughout, allowing you to work slowly and methodically as you initially develop each technique in isolation.
- Pad holder adds in movement, allowing you to incorporate footwork.
- Pad holder places the pads on their chest, presenting the appropriate pad and using broken rhythm to enable you to develop timing, as well as explosive speed, varying the punches according to the position of the pads held.
- Pad holder holds the pad out stationary and attempts to move the pad as you strike. This will

develop your explosive speed and help you to reduce the tell-tale signs that you are about to strike.
- Pad holder attacks back after each technique, either using a single or multiple attacks. Defend against the counters by shielding the attack with your hands and arms, using movement such as footwork, or duck and evade using body movement (*see* Chapter 11 for more information on defending an attack).

Combination Training

With a training partner holding a pair of focus pads, work multiple attacks using each of the techniques detailed in the last section and train them in the following ways:

- Pad holder calls out the names of techniques in multiples of two, three or four, and you respond straight away by performing the appropriate techniques in the same order. Either remain stationary or utilize footwork into the drill.
- Pad holder calls out two, three or four, and you attack using appropriate techniques based on how the pads are held. Either remain stationary or utilize footwork into the drill.

Fig 104 Focus pads held for a jab and a lead elbow.

Fig 105 Focus pads held for a cross and a rear elbow.

Fig 106 Focus pads held for a lead hook and spinning back fist.

Fig 107 Focus pads held for a rear hook and lead back fist.

Fig 108 Focus pads held for a lead uppercut.

Fig 109 Focus pads held for a rear uppercut.

- Using broken rhythm, the pad holder holds out the pads in varying positions and angles for two, three or four attacks, and you strike using the correct techniques until the pads are placed back on the pad holder's chest. Either remain stationary or utilize footwork into the drill.

Power Training

With a training partner holding a kick shield as shown (Figures 110–113), isolate each of the techniques detailed in the last section and train them in the following ways:

- In a stationary position, work each technique in isolation with full power, incorporating the full movement of the body and legs to assist.
- Utilizing footwork and movement, pad holder maintains the same pad position allowing you to work the appropriate techniques with full power.
- In a stationary position, work each technique in isolation with full power for a period of one minute, as many times as possible.

Vary the above training drills by working them for one-minute, two-minute and three-minute

Fig 110 Kick shield held for a jab, cross, lead elbow and rear elbow.

53

rounds with thirty-second, forty-five-second and one-minute rest periods, respectively. As you become more proficient with the techniques and training drills, try working off the opposite lead to develop your weaker side. You can also replace the time count with a repetition count, instead of working for two minutes, look to achieve fifty isolated punches instead. As you become more familiar with these drills, you will no doubt start finding other training methods you can include to further develop your kickboxing routines.

Other great training aids are: punch bags, particularly full-length ones for developing low-level attacks; free-standing bags, which don't have to be wall- or ceiling-mounted; floor-to-ceiling balls; maize balls; and hook and jab bags. Each training aid can be used in much the same way as a pair of focus pads held by a partner; so, if you don't have the luxury of a training partner on a regular basis, then consider one of these other training aids instead.

Fig 111 Kick shield held for lead hooking punch and spinning back fist.

Fig 112 Kick shield held for rear hooking punch and lead back fist strike.

Fig 113 Kick shield held for lead and rear uppercut.

6 Static Kicks

The kicks contained within kickboxing help to put the art alongside many of the other top kicking styles around. Whether training for sport or the street, it is undeniable that a good kicker will have a huge advantage over someone that is not so experienced in this field. Competent kicking does require an incredible amount of dedication as well as training and yet with quality time invested in this area, the end result will almost certainly be worth it.

A competent kicker should, in the right circumstances, out-perform a puncher, as the kicker has the advantage of distance. Kicks are generally used when fighting at long- to mid-range and are used to cover ground and close distance. Punches are more mid- to short-range and generally used after the kicks have bridged the gap. Therefore, a good kicker should be able to use distance, footwork and movement to their advantage, and keep the puncher just out of reach, while still maintaining a good line of attack and defence utilizing the many kicks that the art of kickboxing contains.

The term 'static kick', as in the title of this chapter, basically refers to a kick that is done with the supporting leg on the floor and without incorporating a jump or a spin. In this chapter we will look at the seven static kicks found in kickboxing and include a detailed breakdown of each one, including training drills to help develop them further.

The First Three Basic Kicks

There are three basic kicks that can be found in almost all fighting styles that are not predominantly ground-based arts, and the principle movement and process for each can be very similar in appearance. These are the front kick, round kick and side kick and, as previously mentioned in the preceding chapter, each art may have its own unique twist associated with each technique, therefore the argument could be which one is the most effective. From experience studying many different styles, no one art is solely right. Take an example from one of the many popular sporting combat events, such as cage fighting. Combatants of these events have realized over the years that to train one specific art can be quite limiting; therefore, cross-training has become very popular. This in itself goes to show that no one style has it all. Even arts that claim to have it all, if taken back to their roots, can be seen to take examples and influences from other styles; so once again, study what you want and make it work for you.

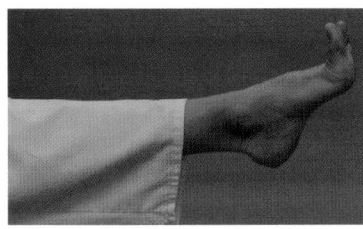

Fig 114 The striking part for the front kick, using the ball of the foot.

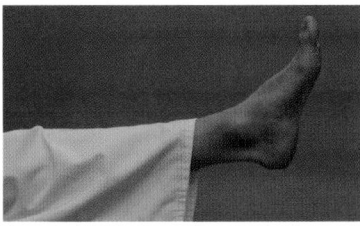

Fig 115 The striking part for the front kick, using the flat of the foot.

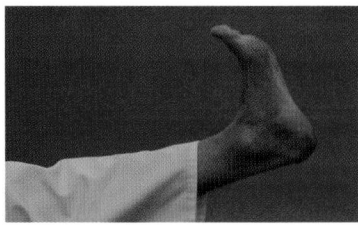

Fig 116 The striking part for the front kick, using the heel.

The Front Kick Off the Lead Leg

This front kick is designed to attack from a front-on position off either the lead or rear leg. You will most commonly see this kick used to attack the mid-section; however, it can also be used to attack the head, as well as the leg. There are three main striking parts that you can use for this kick, namely: the ball of the foot with the foot extended forward (Figure 114); the flat of the foot with the foot held in a vertical position (Figure 115) (designed as a push-kick and used to push an opponent back to gain distance); and the heel with the foot pulled back (Figure 116).

From a front stance (Figure 117), bring the lead leg up into a chambered position (Figure 118) and extend the leg straight out in a stabbing motion, driving the hips through at the same time and striking the target with the correct part of your foot (Figure 119). If your stance is a little wide or your target is further away, you may find it necessary to use your footwork to help centre your balance and cover the distance for this kick.

The Front Kick Off the Rear Leg

The rear leg front kick is the more powerful of the two kicks. However, because it is slightly further away from the target compared to the lead leg, it can be a bit slower and in turn take a little longer to land. Unlike with the lead leg front kick, there is no real necessity to step up as your balance is taken care of by the front leg as the rear leg kick passes through.

From your front-on stance (Figure 120), bring the rear leg up into a chambered position (Figure 121) and, using the hip to add energy to the kick, drive the leg through in a straight line, striking with the correct part of the foot (Figure 122). You can add further distance and energy to this kick by incorporating the hop-step into it and with time and practice, this additional element will enable you to cover great distances with one single movement.

The Lead Leg Round Kick

The round kick is probably the kick that is used more than any other and is a definite favourite with all good kickers. One of the most versatile of all the kicks, it can be used with incredible speed, can deliver knockout power off both the lead and the rear legs and can deliver multiple attacks with ease. Equally effective for high, middle and low use, this kick is definitely one worth mastering. There are many different striking parts associated with the round kick, and which part to be used will depend on the art being studied. For kickboxing, the ball of the foot (Figure 123) or the instep (Figure 124) is favoured; however, the shin is also sometimes used.

From an angled stance (Figure 125), bring the lead leg up into a chambered position and, as you do, slightly pivot on the rear leg, turning the supporting foot out so that the heel of the supporting foot and the knee of the kicking leg both point towards the target (Figure 126). This manoeuvre will assist with your balance and also open up the

Fig 117 In a front stance.

Fig 118 Chamber the lead leg in readiness for the lead kick.

Fig 119 The lead front kick lands.

Fig 120 In a front stance …

Fig 121 … chamber the rear leg in readiness for the rear kick.

Fig 122 The rear front kick lands.

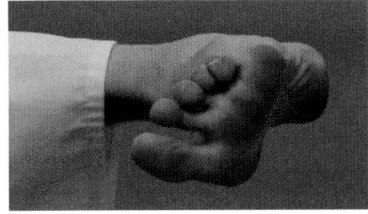

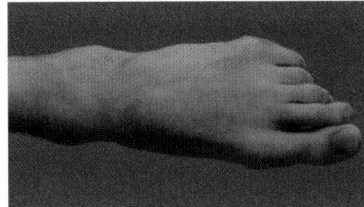

Fig 123 (far left) The striking part for the round kick, using the ball of the foot.

Fig 124 (left) The striking part for the round kick, using the instep.

hips allowing the kick to travel correctly. If the supporting foot is not turned out, you will find that this will put strain on the hip and knee joints, and greatly reduce the energy of the kick. As the leg reaches its chambered position, use the motion of the pivot to extend the leg out, driving with the hips and kicking with the correct part of the foot (Figure 127). Once again, you may wish to add footwork to this kick to cover distance and help centre your balance, if necessary.

Fig 125 In an angled stance …

Fig 126 … leg chambered ready to strike with the supporting foot turned out.

Fig 127 The lead round kick lands.

Fig 128 In a front stance.

Fig 129 Drive the hips round.

Fig 130 The rear leg round kick lands.

The Rear Leg Round Kick

This can be a very powerful kick if done properly but, as with all back leg kicks, does have a tendency to be a little slower to land than the lead leg. Certain styles of kickboxing allow low-level kicking in their syllabus and the rear leg round kick can be an incredibly effective kick when targeted at the thigh region.

From your front stance (Figure 128), drive the hips round in a semicircular motion, pivoting fully on your lead leg this time and use the whole body to generate the energy for this kick (Figure 129). Power through with the kicking leg, following the same line and movement, and strike the target with the correct part of the foot or shin (Figure 130).

The Lead Leg Side Kick

The side kick is a great stopping kick, which essentially means that when used defensively, it can stop an opponent dead in their tracks. The secondary benefit of the side kick, if done properly, is that it puts a barrier between you and the opponent that can be very difficult to get past. It can also be a very fast kick because the motion used to execute the kick is so very different from most others and, when used offensively, it is a great kick to keep an opponent at bay or to use in conjunction with multiple kicks. There are two

Fig 131 The striking part for the side kick, using the side of the foot, known also as the foot sword.

Fig 132 The striking part for the side kick, using the heel.

main striking parts of the foot that you can use for this kick. The first one is the side of the foot, known also as the 'foot sword' (Figure 131), and the second part is the heel with the toes pulled back towards the body (Figure 132).

Fig 133 From a side stance ...   Fig 134 ... chamber the kick.   Fig 135 The lead leg side kick lands.

The side kick can be used from any stance; however, you will probably find it easier and quicker if used from a side-on stance. As an attacking kick it may be necessary to cover distance using one of the steps covered in the chapter on footwork but, as a defensive kick, it will be more effective when done on the spot (or even with a backwards step). From your side-on stance (Figure 133), bring your kicking leg up into a chambered position (Figure 134). Unlike the chambered position of the round kick, the knee of the kicking leg should this time be facing the side wall and the leg should be directly between you and your target. From this position drive the leg forwards using a stabbing motion with the weight of the whole body behind it and strike with the correct part of the foot (Figure 135).

The Rear Leg Side Kick
This kick is favoured a great deal among the traditional kicking arts, such as karate and tae kwon do, and is particularly effective when used for board breaking and destruction. As an attacking kick it is considerably slower than its lead leg equivalent; however, as a power kick it can be quite incredible. One thing to note with this kick is that it is not used a great deal in the freestyle kickboxing world, as the aim of this style of martial 'sport' is speed over power and, as the rear leg side kick has to pass across the lead leg and then move along the exact same line, it is considered to be much quicker and more effective to use a lead leg kick.

From your front stance (Figure 136), bring the rear kicking leg straight up into a chambered position as if performing a rear leg front kick (Figure 137). From this position, pivot on your supporting

Fig 136 In a front stance ...

Fig 137 ... bring the rear leg into a chambered position as used for the front kick.

Fig 138 Pivot to open up the hips and set up the body to execute the side kick properly.

Fig 139 The rear leg side kick lands.

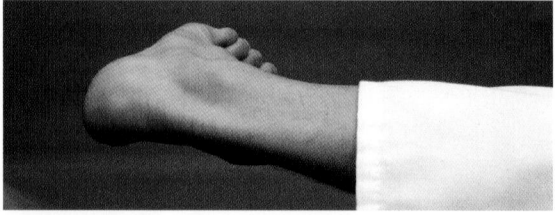

Fig 140 Using the heel as the striking part for the hook kick.

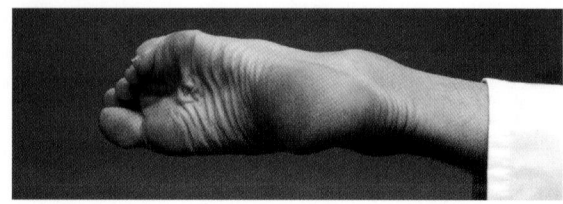

Fig 141 Using the flat of the foot as the striking part for the hook kick.

leg, bringing your kicking leg across your body and your rear supporting foot turned out so that the heel faces your target (Figure 138). Extend the leg out using the same stabbing motion as before, and striking with the correct part of the foot (Figure 139).

The Final Four Static Kicks

The following four kicks form the final part of the static kick syllabus and consist of the hooking kick, the axe kick, the outside crescent kick and the inside crescent kick. These kicks are considered to be slightly more difficult to master than the previous ones, which could be down to several factors. Either the kick may require a higher degree of flexibility in order to work properly or the breakdown of the kick may be slightly more advanced. Either way, they are certainly worth persevering with as they will help to complete your basic knowledge and with practice and training, add additional weapons to your armoury and allow you to attack from different angles and various positions.

The Lead Leg Hooking Kick

This kick is very similar in movement to the lead leg side kick with the added variant of a whip or hooking motion at the end. Due to the way the

kick moves, it is predominately designed to attack the side of the head or body and works very well at high level. It is also a great kick to use in combination with a multiple-kicking attack. The striking part for this kick can either be the base of the heel (Figure 140), which is generally used for destruction, or the flat of the foot (Figure 141), which is usually used when sparring.

From either an angled stance or a side stance, bring your lead leg up into a chambered position (Figure 142). From here, pivot on your supporting leg to open the hips up (Figure 143), extend the leg out just slightly past the target, as if you were performing a side kick (Figure 144), and whip the leg back in, using a hooking motion (Figure 145).

The Rear Leg Hooking Kick

This is probably one of the most awkward and unnecessary kicks within the whole kickboxing syllabus, simply due to the angles that the leg needs to travel in and the shifts in both body mechanics and energy you have to perform in order to get the kick to work. Once you are familiar with the kick and have tried it a few times, you may feel that a lead leg round kick could possibly work a little more efficiently.

Fig 142 Chamber the leg in readiness for the hook kick.

Fig 143 Pivot on the rear leg to open up the hips.

Fig 144 Extend the leg out just past the target.

Fig 145 Hook the leg back in striking with the correct part of the foot.

Fig 146 In a front stance ...

Fig 147 ... chamber the rear leg as if performing a front kick.

Fig 148 Pivot on the supporting leg to open up the hips.

From your front stance (Figure 146), bring the rear leg up into a chambered position, as if you were about to perform a rear leg front kick (Figure 147). From this position, pivot on the supporting leg to open up the hips and turn you side-on (Figure 148). Extend the leg out, in the same way as for the lead leg hooking kick (Figure 149), and as the leg passes the target, hook the kick back in, striking with the correct part of the foot (Figure 150). This one might take a little practise to get right.

Fig 149 Extend the leg out past the target.

Fig 150 Hook the leg back in and land the kick.

Fig 151 In a front stance ...

Fig 152 ... zone out with your rear leg.

Fig 153 Chamber your kicking leg.

Another variation on the rear leg hooking kick involves the use of zoning, as covered in Chapter 4. This allows you to kick off the lead leg but zone out with the rear leg, in such a way that the lead leg becomes the rear leg and you attack the target that is now almost behind you.

From your front stance (Figure 151), zone out at a 45-degree angle transferring your weight on to this leg as you do (Figure 152). Chamber your kicking leg, which should now be your rear leg (Figure 153), and extend the leg out as before (Figure 154), hooking the leg back in towards the target (Figure 155).

Fig 154 Extend the kick out past the target.

Fig 155 Hook the leg back in and land the kick.

The Lead Leg Axe Kick

The axe kick is a technique that does require a good degree of flexibility in order to make it work to its full potential, and if you can invest the time in your stretching here, it will be well worth it. As one of the more intermediate-level static kicks, the axe kick is one of those rare techniques that, if used correctly, can find its target almost every time. It is most effective when used to attack the blind side of your opponent (their lead shoulder), as this shoulder can sometimes obscure the peripheral vision, allowing for a greater likelihood of the kick landing. It should also ideally travel across your body (across your open side), rather than allowing the body to open up by kicking in the reverse direction. The striking part for this kick can be either the heel (Figure 156) or the flat of the foot (Figure 157).

You may find this kick easier to start with if you use a simple shuffle step to generate the momentum. Alternatively, play around with the various stances and footwork steps until you find one that works well for you. From an angular stance (Figure 158), shuffle-step up with your rear foot to cover distance and generate the energy and momentum required for this kick (Figure 159). Using the dynamic movement of the shuffle, pivot on your supporting foot to open up the hips and swing your lead leg straight up, ensuring the kick travels across your body for added protection (Figure 160). As the foot passes over the target, drive it directly down on to the striking area and use the hips to add additional power and energy to the kick (Figure 161).

Fig 158 In an angular stance ...

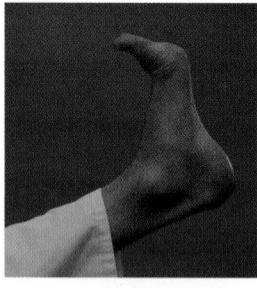

Fig 156 Using the heel as the striking part for the axe kick.

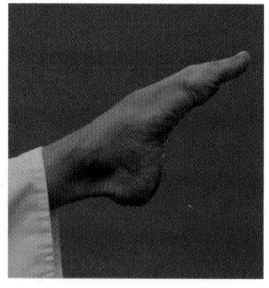

Fig 157 Using the flat of the foot as the striking part for the axe kick.

Fig 159 ... shuffle-step up with your rear foot.

The Rear Leg Axe Kick

Understanding the kick off the rear leg will give you the distinct advantage of being able to use the axe kick to attack the blind side of your opponent, regardless of which leg they have forward. This ability is particularly useful if they have a tendency to switch stance during a fight.

From a front stance (Figure 162), swing your rear leg across your body in the same way as you did for the lead leg, driving the hips through to bring the kicking leg fully forward (Figure 163). Ensure the leg travels above the actual target (Figure 164) and bring the kick down directly on top of the striking area (Figure 165).

Fig 160 (top left) Swing the leg up and pivot at the same time.

Fig 161 (top right) Drive the kick down on to the target.

Fig 162 (right) In a front stance ...

Fig 163 … swing the rear leg up and across the body.

Fig 164 When the kick reaches its highest point …

Fig 165 … drive the leg down on to the target area.

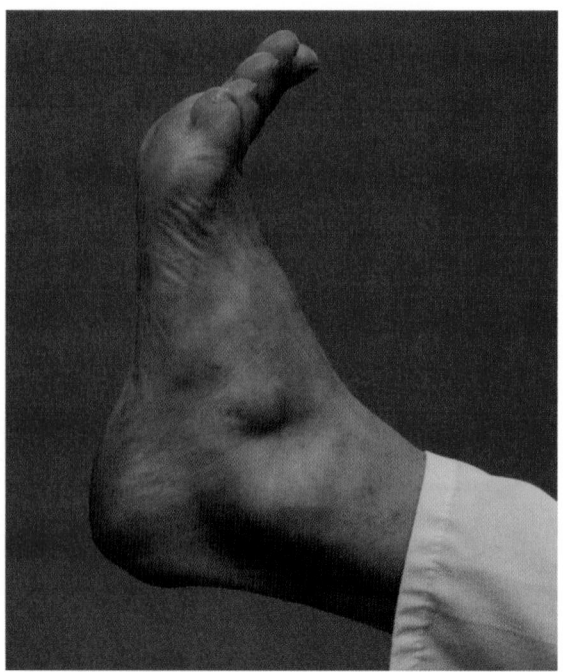

Fig 166 The striking part for the outside crescent kick.

The Lead Leg Outside Crescent Kick

The crescent kicks are simply variations of the axe kick and are designed to travel in a similar way but attack at a different angle. They tend to complement the axe kick quite well and enable the user to quickly switch between angles, based on the movements of the opponent. They can be used from long range with good footwork and can also be used at close range with good flexibility in distances where punches would normally be used. They can also be used as a major attack or to set up a second technique and, due to the nature of the kick, can also be used to attack an opponent's guard, if needed. The striking part for this particular crescent kick is the outside of the heel with the foot held in a vertical position (Figure 166).

From a front or angular stance, shuffle-step up with your rear foot and use this movement to generate the motion and energy required for the kick, as you did with the axe kick (Figure 167). This time, however, instead of bringing the leg straight up and down, you now need to bring the leg around in a crescent motion travelling away from the target initially (Figure 168) and, as the kick reaches the

Fig 167 In your chosen stance, shuffle-step up.

relevant height, drive the leg back in again towards the target, using the hips for energy, and striking with the correct part of the foot (Figure 169).

Fig 168 Swing the lead leg out to the side.

Fig 169 And back in again towards the target.

Fig 170 In a front stance …

Fig 171 … swing the rear leg out to the target line.

Fig 172 Drive the kick back in towards the target.

The Rear Leg Outside Crescent Kick

You may well find the crescent kicks more effective when used to attack the inside of your opponent, as opposed to the outside or the blind side, as in the case of the axe kick. Due to the way the crescent kick travels, it is quite possible that an attempt at a head-height kick via the outside route could be easily absorbed by the opponent by simply raising the lead shoulder to defend the head or by stepping into the kick to deflect it. Admittedly you may still strike the back or shoulder, however, it is unlikely to have the same effect as would a clean shot to the head or body. The rear leg outside crescent kick gives you the advantage of being able to attack the inside of the body without the need for you to switch your stance and give away your intentions.

From a front stance (Figure 170), swing your rear leg across your body in a crescent motion travelling from the inside out (Figure 171). As the kick reaches the target line, drive it back in towards the striking area, kicking with the correct striking part of the foot (Figure 172).

The Lead Leg Inside Crescent Kick

The inside crescent kick is the final static kick and one of the easiest of all to perform. It is designed to attack the inside of your opponent and works equally well to the head or body. It is also the kick that is seen in many martial art movies, being used to parry a straight punch or direct knife attack, although in reality it would be highly inadvisable to try using a kick to do this and for that reason it is probably best left to the movie industry. The only real disadvantage that you may find with this kick is that, due to the way it travels, it does have a tendency to leave you slightly open and vulnerable to attack – so use with caution and a tight guard. The striking part for the inside crescent kick is the inside of the heel with the foot held in a vertical position (Figure 173).

From a front stance (Figure 174), shuffle-step up with your rear leg (Figure 175) and swing your lead leg out to the side of your body in a crescent motion (Figure 176). As your leg reaches the line of the striking area, drive it back in again towards the target, using the hips for additional power and energy (Figure 177).

The Rear Leg Inside Crescent Kick

The principle for this kick is the same as the rear leg outside crescent kick. Understanding the inside crescent kick of both the lead and rear legs gives you the added advantage of being able to attack both quickly and directly with little to no telegraphing of your intentions – a skill sought after by every martial artist or sport fighter in the world.

Fig 174 In a front stance ...

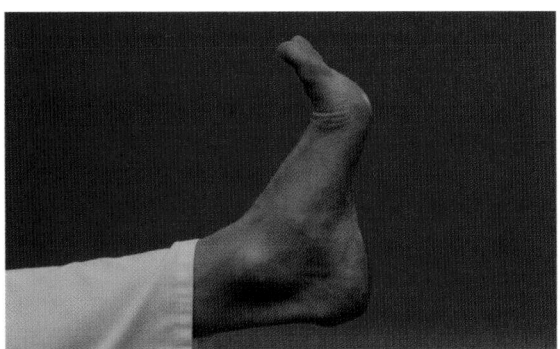

Fig 173 The striking part for the inside crescent kick.

Fig 175 ... shuffle-step up with your rear leg.

69

Fig 176 Swing your lead leg out to the side.

Fig 177 Drive the kick back in towards the target.

From your front stance (Figure 178), transfer your weight on to your lead leg and swing your rear leg out to the side until it reaches the target line (Figure 179). From here, drive the kick back in towards the striking area, attacking with the correct part of the foot (Figure 180).

Fig 178 From your front stance ...

Fig 179 ... swing your rear leg out to the side.

Fig 180 Drive the kick back into towards the target.

Training Drills

With a good understanding of all the kicks covered in this chapter you should now have enough knowledge to be able to attack from both long and close range, and off the lead and rear hand or leg from any angle or stance. This section will now aim to complete your training so far with a series of simple drills with which to develop your kicking ability even further. It is highly recommended that you are fully warmed up, have stretched correctly and wear the appropriate training shoes or foot protectors and training supports, if needed, to prevent the risk of injury before commencing the following training drills.

Resistance Training 1

Strap on a pair of ankle weights, if you have some (the weight of the leg should be sufficient to start with otherwise), and with slow deliberate movements working on each of the three basic kicks (front kick, round kick and side kick), go through the motions of each kick in isolation and as slowly as possible. You should aim to perform each kick for around ten to twelve repetitions and should increase or reduce the weight accordingly to ensure you are achieving this target.

It should take you at least ten seconds to take each kick from your ready position (Figure 181), to chambered position (Figure 182), full extension (Figure 183) and back again (Figure 184). At full extension you should hold the position for a count of three seconds and completely tense your leg muscles as you do. If you find that you are managing to complete each repetition in less than ten seconds, you are kicking too fast. If you have trouble balancing when first starting out, then use a chair or similar support to assist you.

Fig 181 From your starting position use a chair for support.

Fig 182 Bring the leg into a chambered position.

Fig 183 Extend the kick out and hold for three seconds.

Fig 184 Re-chamber and land the leg.

Fig 185 Target the low line.

Resistance Training 2

Once you have spent some time training the basic drills, and your balance has improved to a point where you can competently pull off at least ten slow kicks with ankle weights and no artificial support, then move on to this next training drill. Taking each of the three basic kicks in turn, mark three focus points, low section, mid section and high section, on a target such as a punch bag, wall or similar solid object.

For this drill, your objective is to target the low line and hold for three seconds (Figure 185), re-chamber the leg and slowly kick out to the mid-line and hold for three seconds (Figure 186) and, finally, re-chamber the leg and slowly kick out to the high line and hold for three seconds (Figure 187). Perform these drills exactly as instructed above and contract the leg muscles each time you hold the kick.

NB Word of warning – *never* kick at full speed wearing ankle weights.

Focus-Pad Training

With a training partner holding a pair of focus pads as shown (Figures 188–192), isolate each of the kicks detailed in the last chapter and train them in the following ways:

Fig 186 Target the mid-line.

Fig 187 Target the high line.

Fig 188 Focus pads held for a front kick
and side kick.

Fig 189 Focus pads held for a round
kick, hooking kick and crescent kicks.

Fig 190 Focus pads held for an axe kick.

Fig 191 Focus pads held for round kicks, hooking kicks and crescent kicks off the opposite side.

- Pad holder remains stationary throughout, allowing you to work slowly and methodically, as you initially develop each technique in isolation.
- Pad holder adds in movement, allowing you to incorporate footwork.
- Pad holder places the pads on their chest, presenting the appropriate pad and using broken rhythm to enable you to develop timing as well as explosive speed, varying the kicks according to the position of the pads held.
- Pad holder attacks back after each technique, using either single or multiple attacks. Defend against the counters by shielding the attack with your hands and arms, using footwork or duck and evasion tactics utilizing your body movement.

Combination Training

With a training partner holding a pair of focus pads, work multiple attacks using each of the techniques detailed in the last section and train them in the following ways:

Fig 192 Focus pads held for an axe kick off the opposite leg.

- Pad holder calls out the names of techniques in multiples of two, three or four, and you respond straight away by performing the appropriate techniques in the same order. For this drill, you can either remain stationary or utilize your footwork. This can be kicks in isolation or kick and punch/punch and kick combinations.
- Pad holder calls out two, three or four and you attack using appropriate techniques based on how the pads are held, either stationary or incorporating footwork into the drill.
- Using broken rhythm, the pad holder holds out the pads in varying positions and angles for two, three or four attacks, and you strike using the correct techniques until the pads are placed back on the pad holder's chest, either stationary or incorporating footwork into the drill.

Power Training

With a training partner holding a kick shield as shown (Figures 193–197), isolate each of the kicks detailed in the last section and train them in the following ways:

- In a stationary position, work each technique in isolation with full power, incorporating the full movement of the body and pivot to assist.
- Utilizing footwork and movement, pad holder maintains the same pad position, allowing you to work the appropriate techniques with full power.
- In a stationary position, work each technique as many times as you can, using full power for a period of one minute.

Fig 193 Kick shield held for a front kick and side kick.

Fig 194 Kick shield held for a round kick, hooking kick and crescent kicks.

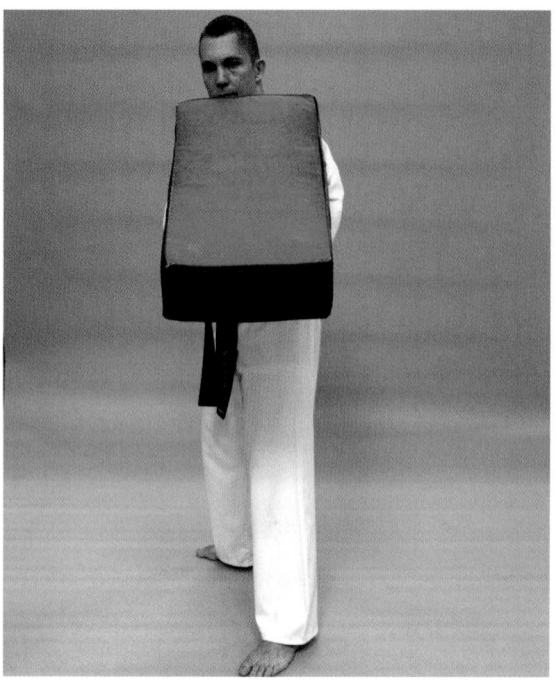

Fig 195 Kick shield held for an axe kick.

Fig 196 Kick shield held for round kicks, hooking kicks and crescent kicks off the opposite side.

Vary the above training drills by working them for one-minute, two-minute and three-minute rounds with thirty-second, forty-five-second and one-minute rest periods, respectively. As you become more proficient with the techniques and training drills, try working off the opposite lead to develop your weaker side. You can also replace the time count with a repetition count, instead of working for two minutes, look to achieve fifty isolated kicks instead. As you become more familiar with these drills, you will no doubt start finding other training methods you can include to further develop your kickboxing routines.

As mentioned previously, if you do not have the luxury of a training partner, then try incorporating other training aids into your routine, such as punch bags, free-standing bags and so on, to achieve the same results.

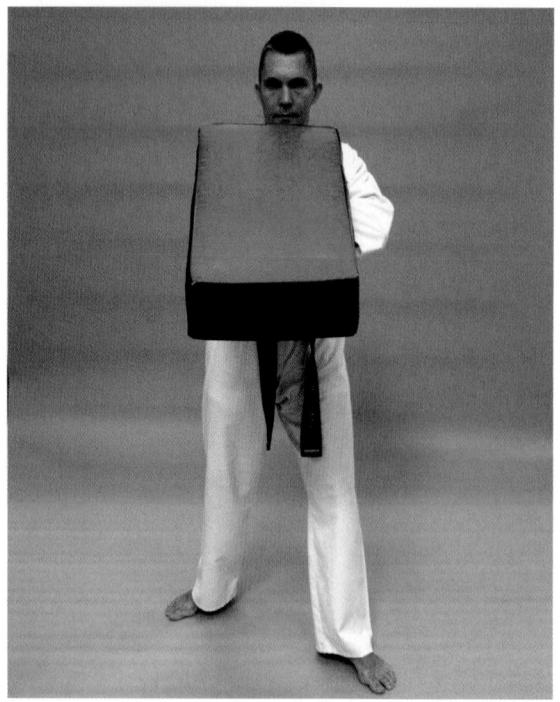

Fig 197 Kick shield held for an axe kick off the opposite side.

7 Multiple Kicks

In this chapter we are going to focus on multiple kicking drills and, by doing so, look at ways with which to use the static kicks taken from the last chapter as efficiently as possible. Using multiple kicks in combination is a skill seen only amongst the greatest kickers and the ability these martial artists have to flow from one kick to another, with grace and ease, comes from nothing more then flexibility and training.

It is very rare, when faced with an experienced opponent, that a single attack will find its mark, and so for that reason combinations of techniques are generally used. The downside for the inexperienced kicker is that the necessity to land the leg after the kick, recover, re-adjust and re-kick, uses up valuable time and energy and can, in a lot of cases, lead to fatigue and/or a successful counter-attack from the opponent. Therefore, to become a successful kicker, you need to understand how to reduce or remove these limitations and, in doing so, change the fight around.

By using multiple kicks in combination and without the need to land the leg and yet still be able to move, follow and attack, while all the time keeping the opponent under pressure, you may force them to make a mistake, of which you can then take advantage. Multiple kicking is one of the most effective ways of adding pressure to a fight and with a little bit of time spent in this area you will certainly see the rewards that can be had.

Popular Combinations

As easy as it may at first appear simply to group kicks together in this manner, this chapter will teach you how to execute the most effective combinations of kicks to ensure they work as efficiently as possible for you and the reasons why certain combinations work when others do not. Don't forget that in order to use multiple kicks effectively, a reasonable level of flexibility is required; so, if you are rushing through this book, then it might be worth slowing down at this point and spending a little bit of time focusing on your stretching and perfecting your basic kicks.

All the kicks featured in this chapter have been detailed in full in the previous chapter, so it is assumed that your understanding of each kick when worked in isolation is fairly proficient.

The Double Round Kick Combo

This combination is designed to set up a clear attack to the head by causing the opponent to draw their guard down in order to protect the body from the first round kick.

In your angular stance (Figure 198), perform a lead leg round kick to the body in order to draw the guard down (Figure 199). As soon as the opponent drops their guard to defend the attack, re-chamber the kick without landing the leg and fire the second kick straight up to the head (Figure 200). The key thing with this combination is to keep the knee high. As you attack the body with the first kick, bring your knee up as high as you can. This will then remove the need for you to raise the knee even further to reach the head, it will help with your balance and it will make the second kick a lot faster. Be sure to keep your guard in place and your body as upright as possible throughout the combination.

The Double Round Kick Training Drill

This training drill will help you to develop the correct movement and body mechanics for the double round kick. Either working with a training partner or using a target of some kind for focus (a punch bag or similar will suffice), support yourself by using a chair or some other

Fig 198 In an angular stance, attack to the body with a lead round kick.

Fig 199 Re-chamber the kick ...

Fig 200 ... and attack the head.

Fig 201 Support yourself using a chair or other sturdy object.

sturdy object (Figure 201). Chamber the leg for the first kick, ensuring you bring your knee up high and pointing towards the target (Figure 202). Strike the body as described previously (Figure 203), re-chamber the leg (Figure 204) and strike to the head (Figure 205).

Fig 202 Chamber the leg for the body kick.

Fig 203 Attack the body.

Fig 204 Re-chamber the leg.

Fig 205 Strike to the head.

Practise this drill for twenty repetitions off each lead (left leg in front for twenty kicks and then right leg in front for twenty kicks). Once you are proficient with this drill, move on to the next drill to help you develop focus and targeting.

The Double Side Kick Combo

This combination can also be used to attack the body and head in the same way as the double round kick combination. Alternatively, it can be used to attack the body and chase a retreating opponent when used in conjunction with the hop-step.

From a side-on stance (Figure 206), chamber the leg for a mid-line side kick (Figure 207). Execute the kick to the body (Figure 208) and, as your opponent steps back and away from the kick, either to avoid the attack or from the force of the blow, re-chamber the kick (Figure 209) and by utilizing the hop-step to cover the distance, use the energy of this forward motion to attack to the mid-line once again (Figure 210). As long as the opponent continues to move backwards in a fairly straight line, you can continue the attack until the kick either lands or they change the angle of their retreat.

Fig 206 In a side stance ...

Fig 207 ... chamber the leg for a mid-line side kick.

Fig 208 Kick to the body.

Fig 209 Re-chamber the kick.

Fig 210 Hop-step forwards and attack once more.

The Double Side Kick Training Drill

Working with a partner holding a kick shield (or, if you are on your own, use a hanging punch bag), step up from your preferred stance and chamber the kick (Figure 211). Execute the side kick towards the mid-line, striking the target with power (Figure 212). As your partner steps back, re-chamber the kick (Figure 213) and strike again using the hop-step to cover the distance (Figure 214).

The Hooking Kick Round Kick Combo

This combination is designed to set up an attack to the head by leading the opponent into a false sense of security and therefore causing them to make the mistake of attempting a counter-strike.

From an angular stance (Figure 215), chamber the leg in preparation for a head-height hooking kick (Figure 216). Attempt the hooking kick, and allow your opponent to lean back out of the way (Figure 217). As the hooking kick passes the target, stop the kick and chamber the leg for a round kick (Figure 218), as the opponent moves in for a counter-strike, attack the head with the round kick (Figure 219).

Fig 211 From your stance, chamber the leg for a mid-line side kick.

Fig 212 Attack to the mid-line.

Fig 213 Re-chamber the kick.

Fig 214 Hop forwards to cover distance and kick again.

Fig 215 From an angular stance …

Fig 216 ... chamber the leg for a hook kick.

Fig 217 Execute the kick.

Fig 218 Re-chamber the kick for a round kick.

Fig 219 Land the round kick.

Fig 220 Chamber the leg for the hooking kick.

Fig 221 Strike the first pad using the correct striking tool.

Fig 222 Re-chamber the leg keeping the knee high.

Fig 223 Attack with the round kick to complete the combination.

The Hooking Kick Round Kick Training Drill
In order to fully benefit from this drill, you will ideally need a training partner holding a pair of focus pads as shown. Alternatively, if you are on your own, a hanging target such as a speed ball or maize ball will work just as well. From your preferred stance, step up with the supporting leg and chamber the leg for the hooking kick (Figure 220). Strike the pad held at head level with the correct striking part of the foot (Figure 221). It would be advisable to simply skim the edge of the pad with this kick instead of hitting the pad full on, as a solid connection at this point will slow the combination down. As the kick passes the centre line, stop the leg and re-chamber the kick, keeping the knee high and in line with the target (Figure 222). Strike to the second pad with the round kick, simulating a kick to the head (Figure 223) and then place the leg back down and step back into your guard. Work this drill for two minutes off the lead leg, change your lead and continue for a further two minutes, using the other leg.

The Round Kick Hooking Kick Combo
This combination starts the more advanced multiple-kicking combinations and requires a greater understanding of balance and body mechanics. It

Fig 225 Kick to the head and allow the opponent to block the attack.

would be advisable to ensure that you are competent with the kicks in isolation before attempting the following multiple kicks.

From your angular stance, chamber the leg for a round kick (Figure 224). Execute the round kick to the head and allow your opponent to defend

Fig 224 Chamber the leg for the round kick.

Fig 226 Adjust the hip position and re-chamber the leg.

Fig 227 Extend the kick out.

Fig 228 Attack with the hooking kick.

Fig 229 Instruct your partner to hold their arm out.

the attack (Figure 225). Then, as you retract the kick, adjust the lead hip position to bring your body slightly further round and re-chamber the leg for a hooking kick (Figure 226). Extend the leg out (Figure 227) and attack to the head with the hooking kick (Figure 228).

The Round Kick Hooking Kick Training Drill
Working with a training partner, instruct them to hold their lead arm out at a height you are comfortable with (Figure 229). Using this as a height guide, attempt to kick just above the arm with the round kick at about 50 per cent of your normal speed (Figure 230). Then retract the kick and adjust the hip position, as described in the previous breakdown (Figure 231). Finally, kick above the arm with the hooking kick at the same speed (Figure 232). This drill will help to develop your balance as well as strengthen the muscles used throughout this combination. It will also allow you to focus on a target without the added pressure of having to actually hit anything, which is important at this stage. Work this drill for two minutes off the lead leg, change your lead and continue for a further two minutes off the other leg.

Fig 230 Kick above the arm at half your normal speed.

Fig 231 Retract the kick and re-adjust.

The Axe Kick Side Kick Combo

This combination works exceptionally well against a counter-fighter, thanks to the side kick's speed and stopping power. As most people find that, if done correctly, the axe kick can be a difficult kick to defend against, when used to set up a second attack, one of three things may happen:

1. Initially the kick may hit the target; therefore, a second attack may not be necessary.
2. The kick can be evaded, either by moving out of the way or ducking underneath. In order for you to keep the knee high and to prevent the leg from hitting the floor and slowing the combination down at this point, strong leg muscles and good balance will be required for this option to work.
3. The kick can be blocked; either by the opponent's lead shoulder or their forearm in the case of a rising style block with their front arm. This defence will allow you to use their body as a springboard in order to bounce the leg back off again and set up the side kick.

In the case of the last two possibilities, the tendency, once the opponent thinks the axe kick is on its way to the floor, is to rush in for a counter-attack; this is when the second kick is most dangerous.

Fig 232 Execute the hooking kick slightly above target.

From your angular stance, step up to cover the distance, centre your balance and generate the momentum required for the axe kick (Figure 233). Swing the lead leg up, as previously described, to execute the first kick (Figure 234).

As the axe kick does its job, retract the leg, keeping the knee high and at the same time pivot on the rear foot and chamber the leg ready for the side kick (Figure 235) and then execute the kick (Figure 236).

Fig 233 Step up to generate the momentum required for the axe kick.

Fig 234 Execute the axe kick in the normal way.

Fig 235 Retract the leg and set up for the side kick.

Fig 236 The side kick lands.

Axe Kick Side Kick Training Drill

For this training drill, you ideally need a partner holding a kick shield or use a punch bag if you are on your own. When holding a kick shield for an axe kick, angle the shield slightly, as shown; this will cause the kick to act in the same way as it does when kicking the body (Figure 237). Step up and execute the axe kick in the normal way, hitting the pad with the heel or flat of the foot (Figure 238). Retract the kick, as before, and ensure the pad holder straightens the kick shield (Figure 239); hit the pad with the side kick (Figure 240). If the opponent steps back after the axe kick, then simply use a hop-step to cover the distance and add extra energy to the kick. Work this drill for two minutes off the lead leg, change your lead and continue for a further two minutes.

Side Kick Axe Kick Combo

This one may well be the most difficult to master, as it does require a good level of muscle development as well as control, in order to perform the second kick with speed. It is also a very effective double-kick combo, as it is unexpected and can also be grouped together with the double side kick

Fig 237 Square up to the kick shield and ensure it is held at a slight angle.

combo, allowing you to chase an opponent and switch the kick mid flow, in order to confuse.

Fig 238 Hit the pad with the axe kick using the heel or flat of the foot.

Fig 239 Retract the kick and straighten the target.

Fig 240 Strike the pad with the side kick.

From your side stance, execute the side kick to the mid-line, as normal (Figure 241). If the kick lands either to the body or the guard, then bounce the foot off the mark and, as you bring the leg back, pull the knee up high (Figure 242). Use the momentum of this movement to straighten the leg, so the kick reaches its highest point (Figure 243), and drive the axe kick down on to the target, striking with the correct part of the foot (Figure 244).

Side Kick Axe Kick Training Drill
Ideally, you need a partner holding a single focus pad at a slight angle, as shown (Figure 245). Perform the side kick either pulling the kick short of your partner, utilizing the leg muscles to set up the axe kick, or touch your partner on the arm and use this as a spring board (alternate between the two) (Figure 246). As you retract the leg from the first kick, set up the leg for the second kick, as previously described (Figures 247 and 248), and drive the kick down on to the focus pad to develop your targeting (Figure 249). Work this drill for two minutes off the lead leg, change your lead and continue for a further two minutes.

Fig 241 Side kick to the mid-line.

Fig 242 Bounce the kick off the body and pull the knee up high.

Fig 243 Use the momentum to straighten the leg …

Fig 244 … and drive the axe kick down towards the target.

It is worth persevering with these multiple-kicking combos as they will certainly improve your sport-fighting ability over time. However, don't be tempted to rush ahead of the programme and 'run before you can walk'. Remember the golden rule of foundation building, as covered in Chapter 4. Ensure your static kicks are of a high enough level to successfully adapt and make the transition into a multiple-kick combo. If not, then there's a good chance you will fall at the first hurdle and this is the last thing you want to happen in the middle of a fight.

The point at which you know you have reached the required level, is the point at which you are in control of your kicks and not when your kicks are still in control of you. When you are able to kick a target exactly where you want, without losing balance, and land the leg again with complete control of the technique from start to finish, you are ready to move on to the multiple-kicking section. Until then, persevere with the basics, as these are the areas that will build the strong foundations for you.

Fig 245 With a partner holding a focus pad, as shown…

As you become more confident with the double kicks, speed and power will start to increase naturally. You can also encourage your training partner to move around in order to add a bit more realism to the drills. Try incorporating more than one double-kick combo in the two-minute drills, and remember to always start off slowly and gradually increase the speed and height of the kicks, once you become comfortable with the drill.

Fig 246 ... side kick to the mid section.

Fig 247 Bounce the leg off the body.

Fig 248 Chamber for the axe kick.

Fig 249 Drive the axe kick down on to the target.

8 Spinning Kicks

Spinning kicks are by far the most impressive of all the techniques we have currently looked at and with a good understanding of speed and timing these can be used with incredible effect. There is much debate, however, as to the effectiveness of the spinning kick in a combat situation and, indeed, in the hands of the inexperienced fighter, they may not be all that effective. As with anything though, the more you practise something the better it becomes and although the argument falls in the favour of the basic technique, it can't be denied that in the hands of a skilled kicker, the spinning kick can be quite an incredible weapon.

There are many spinning kicks available to the kickboxer, although some are more common than others. In this chapter we will look at the most popular kicks that can be used and also take a journey into the world of the lesser-seen spinning kick, with breakdowns and training drills to help you get the best out of each technique.

Popular Spinning Kicks

All of the static kicks covered so far can be turned into spinning kicks if needed and, indeed, through trial and error, this is what tends to happen in the world of martial arts (don't forget, every martial arts technique known to man or woman has, at some point, been invented by someone). However, there are some spinning kicks that work better than others, and some that are a lot easier to perform, which might explain why you may only ever see the favourites performed instead of the full repertoire.

As powerful as a spinning kick can be, one key thing to remember is that in order to perform one of these techniques, there is going to be a requirement for you to turn your back on your opponent. This is always going to be a risky manoeuvre

as, for a split second, you are blind and, therefore, vulnerable and an experienced opponent may well take advantage of this fact. You also run the risk of the technique being defended, particularly with circular spinning techniques, like the reverse round kick or the spinning hook kick, due to the amount of time it takes for the kick to land. And, finally, even if you are skilled enough to avoid the last two challenges, there is always the problem of a counter-attack as you come out of the spin, as this is the point at which your main focus is going to be on the landing and the recovery from the spin, and there's a good chance you may be slightly off-balance. So, in conclusion, spinning kicks look great, but in order to make them effective in a combat situation, you will need to invest a great deal of time and effort in this particular area.

To begin this section we're going to focus on the more commonly seen spinning kicks, as these may be the ones you are most familiar with, which will also make them easier to grasp. Once you are competent with these, then try moving on to the final set of spinning kicks at the end of the chapter.

The Spinning Back Kick

Without a doubt, the spinning back kick is one of the most powerful techniques in the martial arts and is capable of delivering over 1,500lb (700kg) of force. It is a technique that originally started out as a spinning side kick, however, due to the weakness of the spinning side kick in competition (as it leaves the user open to a counter-attack during the spinning stage), the spinning back kick was developed.

The striking part for this technique is the same as for the side kick (the heel or the foot sword), and the foot is held in exactly the same position. It is ideally used to attack front-on and works equally as well at close range as it does at a distance. It is also both an excellent defensive and offensive technique that can stop an opponent dead in their tracks.

Despite it's name, if you actually do spin with this kick you are likely to get it wrong, as the footwork for the spinning back kick actually requires more of a twist than a spin. This is also the most common reason why many people struggle with this particular spinning kick. For the ease of understanding, we'll demonstrate this technique in a left lead, kicking with the right (rear) leg. If possible, while you are perfecting this kick, try to find yourself a straight line on the floor that you can use as a guide. It's not essential, but it will help prevent any mistakes being made in the early stages.

From an angular stance facing forwards (Figure 250), twist your feet so that your whole body now faces the other direction and your target is behind you (Figure 251). Ensure that as you twist, your rear foot (which now becomes your front foot) is moved clear of your back leg otherwise this leg will

act as a natural obstacle and hinder the effectiveness of the kick. Turn your head so that you can look over your right shoulder to ensure the target hasn't moved (Figure 252). Slide the right leg back along the floor in a completely straight line (this simple manoeuvre will ensure that the kick hits the target dead centre and will prevent the spin-off effect that occurs when the body mechanics are wrong) (Figure 253), and as the leg passes your body, lift it up and strike the target using the heel or foot sword (Figure 254).

The temptation for many people is to drop their guard when performing kicks. This is a bad habit to get into and one that can be difficult to break once the foundations have been set, so avoid doing this at all costs. Remember to also focus on the position of the foot to ensure the kick works to its maximum. The foot of the supporting leg should be facing away from the target at this stage to ensure the body mechanics are correct. Once the kick has connected, you can choose to either land the leg in front for a possible second attack or to step back into your original stance.

Fig 250 From an angular stance ...

Fig 251 ... twist your feet so your target is directly behind you.

Fig 252 Look over your shoulder.

Fig 253 Bring the leg back in a completely straight line.

Fig 254 Strike the target with the correct part of the foot.

The Reverse Round Kick

There are many different names for this kick and each one will differ depending on the art studied or the country you live in. Regardless of what you choose to call it, the elements of the kick will no doubt remain the same and, for that reason, this kick can be found in many other fighting arts, due to its versatility and effectiveness.

The striking part for this kick is the same as for the hooking kick (the base of the heel or the flat of the foot), and it is best performed from either a side-on stance or an angular stance. It is also designed for attacking the side of an opponent and, due to the motion of the kick, it is an incredibly powerful technique. It can be used low, mid or high section and, therefore, can be adapted for use by almost anyone, regardless of flexibility.

For the ease of understanding, we'll demonstrate this kick in a left lead, kicking with the right (rear) leg. From your preferred stance (Figure 255) twist your feet so that your whole body now faces the other direction and your target is behind

Fig 255 From your preferred stance ...

Fig 256 ... twist your feet so you face the other direction.

Fig 257 Start the kick.

Fig 258 Keep the leg locked straight.

Fig 259 The leg travels in a circular motion from the floor to its mark.

you (Figure 256). As you start to spin, use the energy created from this momentum to lift your kicking leg off the floor (Figure 257). Keep the leg locked straight and allow it to travel in a completely circular line (Figure 258), and whip your hips and upper body round to add additional energy to the kick and at the same time drive the kicking leg through to find its target (Figure 259).

Once you have executed the kick, try to land with the kicking leg back where it came from in order to put you back into your original lead. You will also find that this will help should you wish to execute a second technique, as well as assisting you with your balance. Keep the leg straight throughout the kick and ensure you keep your body as upright as possible. Finally, keep the guard tight throughout and avoid the common mistake people tend to make with this kick, by dropping the rear hand and leaving the face unprotected.

The Spinning Hook Kick

This kick is an enhancement of the previous one (the reverse round kick) and was developed in order to produce a spinning circular kick that didn't have the restrictions of a straight leg kick. When the leg remains straight, the speed of the spin is slightly reduced, allowing for a greater opportunity to counter-attack. Plus, the locked position of the leg can also make the kick somewhat cumbersome to execute. The spinning hook kick allows the body to spin at a much faster rate by keeping the leg coiled until the very last minute; additional energy is added to the technique through the whipping motion at the end.

As with the last kick, this one is also designed to attack the side of the body with the same striking tools. From an angular or side stance (Figure 260), twist your feet so that your whole body now faces the other direction and your target is behind

Fig 260 From your preferred stance …

Fig 261 … twist your body round and look over your shoulder to line up the kick.

Fig 262 Start the spin and bring the knee up high.

Fig 263 Whip your hips and body round and extend the leg.

Fig 264 Just before the kick lands, hook the leg through.

you; be sure to look over your right shoulder for focus at this point (Figure 261). As you start the spin, lift your rear foot off the floor keeping your knee high (Figure 262). Whip your hips and upper body round and extend the leg out towards the target (Figure 263) and hook the leg through to add the extra energy to the kick (Figure 264).

As with all the spinning kicks covered in this chapter, try landing back in your original stance once the kick is complete and keep the guard tight at all times. Also, notice the position of the supporting foot at the main point of contact (Figure 263). The most common mistake people make is to not fully understand how the supporting leg works. In order to get the body in the correct position for the kick to have the maximum effect, make sure the heel of the supporting foot faces the target. This will open up the hips and assist greatly with your balance. Otherwise you may find that your body mechanics are not correct, resulting in an inferior kick.

The Spinning Axe Kick

The spinning axe kick is generally used for attacking either the front of the opponent in a downward manner or, if done correctly, due to the motion of the kick it can also be used to attack the opponent at an angle, as demonstrated in Chapter 6. It is normally used for a high-section attack (unless the opponent is bent over) and, as such, flexibility is key with this technique. The principles for the spinning axe kick are the same as for the static version, striking with the heel or the flat of the foot, and it is most effective when used to attack the blind side of an opponent. As such, it is a great technique to use against a fighter that prefers an opposite lead to yours, or one that switches lead throughout the fight, as you no longer need to switch with them in order to attack their blind side.

From your preferred stance (Figure 265), twist your feet so that your whole body now faces the other direction and your target is behind you, looking over your shoulder for focus at this point (Figure 266). As you start the momentum of the spin, lift your rear foot off the floor, keeping your knee high to assist with the motion of the kick (Figure 267). Extend the leg as you continue the spin (Figure 268) and, as you turn to face the opponent, drive the kick down in a vertical motion, adding extra energy to the final stage of the kick (Figure 269).

Due to the awkwardness of this kick, it is paramount to understand the control required to bring the leg up, hold it and drive it down. For speed purposes, keep the knee bent as you spin and only straighten it as you start the turn to face the opponent. The kick needs to be at such a height that it will pass over your opponent's shoulder as you spin; otherwise it is likely to hit the shoulder or miss altogether, especially if you are too far away. Once you reach the centre line, stop the spin and drive the kick straight down.

Intermediate Level Spinning Kicks

This next section focuses on spinning kicks that don't tend to get seen that much, unless you are particularly into your kicking arts. This isn't to say that they are not as effective as the ones we have

already looked at, as everything is effective in the right hands. It might just be that the transition through the various stages of the kick may be a little slower than some of the other kicks, which of course will limit their effectiveness and impact. Or it could simply be that times have changed and kicks that may have been prominent many years ago have evolved into much more efficient kicks for the modern-day arena.

The Spinning Round Kick

This particular spinning kick is good for covering distance and works equally well when aimed at the body, as well as to the head. The striking part is the same as for the round kick, the instep or the ball of the foot, and the kick is designed to attack the side of the body in a circular motion. As with most spinning kicks, the faster you spin the more effective the kick; so to increase the speed of attack, this one works well from an angular stance or a side stance.

From your preferred stance (Figure 270), step through with your rear leg so the leg lands in front but your body stays facing the same direction (Figure 271). From here, begin to unwind the body in preparation for the kick and get your head round as fast as possible, so you don't lose sight of your opponent (Figure 272). Start the spin and chamber the leg as you do so (Figure 273), and as the spin winds out, use the momentum you will have generated at this point to land the kick with power (Figure 274).

Naturally, the further through you bring the rear leg at the start of the kick, the further forwards you will travel, so this kick can be used very effectively to cover distance, as well as to generate a great deal of speed due to the wind-up motion at the start.

The Spinning Outside Crescent Kick

As mentioned in the chapter on static kicks, the crescent kicks were originally designed for close-range fighting and the spinning versions are no exception to this rule. They are also unique in the fact that they are the only spinning kicks where the body is kept upright throughout, and it's because of this reason they work exceptionally well when used at close range. The only downside you may find

Fig 265 From your preferred stance ...

Fig 266 ... twist your body round and look over your shoulder.

Fig 267 Use the momentum of the spin to bring the knee up high.

Fig 268 Straighten the leg as you face the target.

Fig 269 Drive the leg down on to the target with the correct striking part.

Fig 270 From your preferred stance …

Fig 271 … bring your rear leg through to the front.

Fig 272 Start the spin.

Fig 273 Chamber the leg …

Fig 274 … and kick the target with the correct striking part.

with this kick is that to generate the power required for this kick to be effective, the body needs to fully rotate, which then momentarily leaves it susceptible to a counter-attack, unlike with the spinning hook kick, for instance, where the body and head are a good distance away from the opponent throughout the technique. As such, you don't tend to see spinning crescent kicks used any more, as fighters have become better at reading them and, therefore, more able to avoid or counter them.

The striking part for this kick is the outside of the foot, as used for the outside crescent kick in Chapter 6, and the kick works better from an angular or side stance. To help you understand the body movement required for the spin, you need to imagine you have a pole running vertically through the centre of your body (from head to toe) and into the ground. This will help you to maintain the correct body position throughout the full movement of this kick. From your preferred stance (Figure 275), start a clockwise spin, keeping the body as upright as possible (Figure 276). Whip the head round to look over your opposite shoulder and focus on the target as you continue the spin (Figure 277). Transfer your balance and your body weight to your lead (left) leg,

which now acts as a pivot (Figure 278), and, as your right shoulder comes into line with the target, start to lift your kicking leg off the floor (Figure 279). Ensure you maintain the spin all the way round, enabling the kick to find its mark (Figure 280). Land the leg back to where it came from, putting you into your left lead once more.

If done correctly, the speed and momentum of the initial spin will cause the leg to whip through. All you need to do is control your balance, maintain the spin and land your foot back down again after the kick finds the target. You may also find that your supporting leg bends slightly when you kick and/or you rise up on to the ball of your foot. This is perfectly natural when performing this type of kick, as the supporting leg will act like a shock absorber and help your balance and rotation. It is also quite possible that your kicking leg will bend as you start the kick. Again, this is perfectly normal, providing the kick is fully extended at the point of impact. If done correctly, the leg will straighten on its own as the spin reaches maximum velocity. Don't bring the kicking leg off the floor until the absolute last second. This will speed up the kick and help with your balance. This completes a 360-degree spinning outside crescent kick.

Fig 275 From your preferred stance ...

Fig 276 ... spin clockwise, keeping the body upright.

Fig 277 Whip the head round to look over the opposite shoulder.

Fig 278 Transfer your body weight to your lead leg.

Fig 279 Start lifting the foot off the floor.

Fig 280 Drive the kick towards its target.

The Spinning Inside Crescent Kick

The principle for this kick is similar to the last one but using the inside part of the foot to attack with this time (as with the inside crescent kick covered in Chapter 6), and an additional step added to compensate for the change of striking tool. The spinning inside crescent kick relies on momentum from the spin to generate the power for the kick and, at the same time, to cover distance; therefore, the spin for this particular technique is of great importance.

In a left lead working from either an angular or side stance (Figure 281), twist your body backwards (Figure 282) so you land with your rear leg in front (Figure 283). As you land, use this leg (the one you have just landed in front) as a pivot and continue the spin so that your left leg starts its return to the front, chambering the leg at the same time (Figure 284). As the kick reaches the centre line, straighten the leg to ensure the kick hits with its full potential (Figure 285) and allow the energy of the kick to continue through, landing the leg naturally and going back into your stance.

As you start the spin, be sure to look over your shoulder to enable you to focus on the target, as demonstrated in Figure 282. You may also find that, as the kick lands, your rear supporting leg

Fig 281 In a left lead, working from an angular or side stance.

Fig 282 Twist your body backwards.

Fig 283 Land the rear leg in front.

Fig 284 Continue the spin and
chamber the kick.

Fig 285 Straighten the leg and strike
with the correct part of the foot.

may bend slightly. This again is a natural part of this kick, as the rear leg acts like a shock absorber in the same way as it does for the previous kick. As long as it doesn't affect your balance, it shouldn't actually hinder the kick in any way.

The Final Contenders

The last three spinning kicks are probably the least seen or the least studied of all the spinning kicks available to the kickboxer, but despite this, they are certainly worth having as part of your kickboxing arsenal. As you progress through your study of kickboxing, you will probably start to favour certain techniques that work better for you. This is a natural part of the development and you will probably find that with such an extensive repertoire of techniques available, what works well for you isn't necessarily going to work well for someone else. This could be down to a number of contributing factors, such as body shape, flexibility, height, strength, natural ability and so on.

However, the golden rule is to learn everything and then focus on what works best for you; that way you end up with a small number of techniques that you can perform well, as opposed to a large number of techniques that you perform adequately. So, study the last three kicks and see how you get on with them, as, realistically, that is the only way you are going to find out.

The Spinning Front Kick

Due to the nature of the kick, the spinning front kick is generally used for attacking the front of the body. It is designed for a mid-section attack but can also be used for a high- or a low-level attack as well. There are two main parts of the foot that you can use to strike with for this kick, as detailed in Chapter 6: the ball of the foot with the foot fully extended, or the heel with the foot pulled back. You may also wish to use the flat of the foot if the kick is to be used as a front push kick. There are several ways to work this kick and we'll look at each one in turn.

Fig 286 In your preferred stance ...

Fig 287 ... step behind with your rear leg.

Fig 288 Twist your body round to unwind.

Fig 289 Chamber the leg.

Fig 290 Strike with the correct part of the foot.

From your preferred stance (Figure 286), step behind your front leg with your rear leg, so that the rear leg lands in front but your body stays facing the same direction, a bit like performing a cross-step (Figure 287). Twist the body round to unwind yourself so you once again face the target (Figure 288). Chamber the leg (Figure 289) and execute the front kick, striking with the correct part of the foot (Figure 290).

Version 2

In this second version, instead of stepping through with your rear leg, as you did for the last kick, we're now going to use the rear leg to kick with. You may actually find this version slightly tricky at first due to the way you spin, stop and kick. However, a little practise and a lot of perseverance will help. In your preferred stance (Figure 291), use your front leg to pivot on and twist your body backwards, looking over your shoulder at the same time (Figure 292). As you do, bring the kicking leg into a chambered position (Figure 293), continue the spin so you once again face the target (Figure 294) and execute the kick (Figure 295).

Fig 291 In your preferred stance …

Fig 292 … pivot backwards using the front leg.

Fig 293 Bring the kicking leg into a chambered position.

Fig 294 Spin all the way around to face the target.

Fig 295 Strike the target with the rear leg.

When you complete the initial spin, be sure to land the rear leg clear of the kicking leg, otherwise this may obstruct the kick when it's in mid-flow. Despite the height of your intended attack, ensure you bring the knee up high and stab the kick out, in order to penetrate the target. This should be different to how you would kick a football, and more of a thrusting or stabbing motion using the hips. Keep the guard high and ensure it moves with the kick; the left hand should be on the chin and the right hand out in front when the right leg is in front but, as you kick with the left leg, the right hand moves to the chin and the left hand moves out.

The Spinning Side Kick
As with the spinning front kick, this kick is also most effective when used to attack the mid-section. The motion for this kick is very similar to the motion used for the spinning back kick, except that you take the spin a quarter-turn further, which puts you into a side-on position, rather than a reverse position. The striking part is the same as for a standard side kick and the leg moves in much the same way, once the spin is complete. Because

you spin further round for this kick, it might be worth starting in more of a side stance rather than a front stance, as this will be easier to begin with and also reduce the time it takes to complete the spin. There are also two versions of this kick and we will look at both in turn.

From a side stance in a left lead (Figure 296), keep the feet where they are and twist your body all the way around in a clockwise motion, so that the right shoulder faces the target (Figure 297). Bring the kicking leg up into a chambered position (Figure 298) and extend the leg out in a perfectly straight line, striking the target with the correct part of the foot (Figure 299) and landing back in your stance.

Version 2
In the last version we used the rear leg to kick with. This time we are going to perform a spinning side kick but strike with the lead leg instead. This second example will also allow you to use the kick from a greater distance and has the added advantage of enabling you to instantly switch between either style, based on the reaction of your opponent.

Working from a side-on stance in a left lead once again (Figure 300), this time use the front foot as a pivot and spin in a clockwise motion, so you land the rear leg in front (Figure 301). Using the motion of the spin, bring the left leg (which will now be your rear leg) into a chambered position (Figure 302) and continue to spin, so your kicking leg lines up with the target and your body is now side-on once again (Figure 303). From here extend the kick straight out towards the target, striking with the correct part of the foot (Figure 304).

The Spinning Back Round Kick
This is probably the most awkward of all the spinning kicks to master, which is why we have saved it until last. By now you should be fairly comfortable with spinning and, up to this point, the spins and the kicks should have complemented each other and fitted together quite nicely. With the spinning back round kick this all changes. It is a spinning kick in the true sense of the word, however, what you have with this kick is two opposite forces working together – a spin travelling in one direction and a kick travelling in the other. For this reason it may

Fig 296 In a left lead, working from a side stance …

Fig 297 … twist your body backwards.

Fig 298 Chamber the kick.

Fig 299 Strike the target.

Fig 300 In a left lead, working from a side stance ...

Fig 301 ... pivot on the front foot and spin the body round backwards.

Fig 302 Chamber the kicking leg as you start the spin.

Fig 303 Spin out so you are once again side-on.

Fig 304 Kick the target with the correct striking part of the foot.

be one of the harder of the spinning kicks to master and may need a little more time dedicated to it.

Don't be put off by this, however, as it is a very effective kick and the motion of the spin combined with the trajectory of the kick can lead an opponent into a false sense of security and force them to make a mistake, which can end in your favour. As with the previous round kicks we have looked at, the striking part of the foot is the same; however, you may just find the instep a little easier to use with this one when first starting off.

From either an angular stance or a side-on stance (Figure 305), start to twist the body backwards as if performing a spinning back kick (Figure 306). As you turn your back on your opponent, look over the lead shoulder to focus on the target (Figure 307) and from this reverse position, bring your kicking leg through on a perfectly straight line and chamber the leg (Figure 308). From here it's just a simple case of snapping the kick out towards the target and striking with the correct part of the foot (Figure 309).

Fig 305 From your preferred stance ...

Fig 306 ... start twisting the body backwards.

Fig 307 Look over your lead shoulder.

Fig 308 Kick through to the front in a straight line.

As you will see when you practise this kick, due to the way the body spins, the opponent is fooled into thinking a spinning hook kick or similar directional attack is on its way. As they prepare to defend the appropriate side of the body, the defences on the other side are often relaxed, which is of course where the kick actually lands.

Training Drills

By this point your training should be progressing well and you should be fairly competent with regards to training the techniques covered so far. Your main training aids should be a punch bag, either free-standing or fixed, a kick shield, a pair of focus pads and a partner. Naturally you can invest in as much high-tech training equipment as your budget will allow, but without going too overboard, a good, full-length punch bag will do the job all on its own, if a training partner is not available to you and, if you have space to hang or store it, it will be available to train with at a moment's notice, any time you are ready. What the punch bag can't offer, however, is feedback and movement,

Fig 309 Strike the target with the correct part of the foot.

and although you can dance round it all day long, it is still pretty stationary and, of course, won't hit you back. Along with the training drills already covered in this book, below are some new drills that you can try to incorporate into your training, using all of the punches and kicks detailed so far.

Shadowing

When developing the spinning kicks a degree of shadowing (or shadow work as it is also known) is important. Shadowing simply involves practising the techniques in mid-air against an imaginary opponent. Anytime a mid-air kick or punch is used, it is advisable to reduce the speed and power slightly so as to avoid any long-term damage that could occur through snapping out the joints. The occasional little burst of speed may not hurt but the occasional little burst of speed over ten years may take its toll. So, the best advice when shadowing, is to focus more on technique rather then speed and power.

Work through each of the spinning kicks covered in this chapter and shadow them for between one and five minutes, depending on your level of fitness. Although you probably won't be out of breath at the end of a shadowing session, your muscles may well be tired if you are not yet used to the training, so adjust your time according to how you feel as you shadow. As a complete beginner to this type of training, it might be advisable to start off for one minute in a left lead, rest for thirty seconds and shadow the same technique again for another minute off the right lead. As you grow stronger, increase the time in durations of thirty seconds and in turn increase the rest period in durations of fifteen seconds – providing, of course, you don't cool down too much as you rest.

Mirror Work

The mirror is a great training aid and, if you have access to a full-length one, as found in most gyms, then certainly take advantage of it. What the mirror will do is give you feedback. You, of course, need to interpret the feedback and make the necessary adjustments to improve your techniques. However, most people that use the mirror as a training aid are surprised at how truthful it can be.

For mirror work, you remain fairly stationary and perform each technique at the same speed as you would when shadowing but observe your every movement. Notice how you hold your guard, where the gaps in your defences are, how your footwork complements the technique, how your body moves, how you land and recover. Basically, put yourself in the shoes of your opponent, as you will effectively be seeing what they see. Also, be your best critic. Be truthful to yourself and, if you think there is need for improvement, then work on the areas that are weak, as this will help to strengthen the overall technique and, as always, build good solid foundations.

Video Camera

This training method can be used in conjunction with the previous two or, if a mirror is not available to you, set up a camcorder or similar recording device and video your training instead. You can then watch and review your performance and, in the same way as with the mirror, record the areas you need to develop and make a conscious effort to work on these at your next training session. As you begin training with a video camera, start off simply by working individual techniques at different angles. This will give you an advantage over the mirror, as you can see how you move from all angles. Start your drills off by facing the camera. Then you can repeat the same drill but this time face left, then right and then backwards.

Once you become comfortable with this type of training, you can start to video any bag work you do and even introduce it when working with a partner. Many competitive fighters will video their training sessions and use this to help them improve. And don't forget that every sports person will almost certainly video their tournaments and competitions and use this to review and improve their performance, or perhaps even review the performance of their competitors, for potential bouts in the future.

Smash Boards

Smash boards (or break boards) are a great way of developing targeting. They are designed to work along similar lines to the karate or tae kwon do wood-breaking power tests that are often seen at demonstrations or competitions, and are a great way of ensuring your technique is correct.

Unlike a block of wood, which will generally break regardless of where you strike it, the smash boards will only break along the centre line. Therefore, unless you connect exactly on this mark, using the correct striking part and correct technique, there is a very high probability that the board won't break. The advantage the user then has with a successful break is that, unlike wood, these boards can be slotted back together again and used once more.

When using a smash board use a sturdy framed holder that in turn is either wall-mounted (ideal when training alone) or supported by a training partner. These holders aren't cheap, mainly because they are not sold all that regularly so the price remains quite high and, although it is possible for someone to hold the smash board for you, they run the risk of getting fingers injured or broken, and most of the time are unable to hold the smash board as rigidly as a frame or holder can, therefore a great deal of energy is lost when the arms of the person holding them buckle. Smash boards are certainly worth investing in, as not only do they offer a great training aid, they can also be great fun and, if you are unable to invest in a holder as well, it might be worth commissioning someone to make one for you or asking several people to hold the boards for you, otherwise you might just be wasting your money.

The colours vary depending on the make of smash board you buy, however, you need to consider that there are varying degrees of toughness ranging from beginner (easy), to intermediate (for the more experience student), through to advanced (very hard). A common practice, once the advanced board becomes too easy to break, is to group two boards together. This adds a whole new perceptive on this type of training method and will certainly ensure your technical ability and targeting reaches a new level. Just be sure the holder you purchase can accommodate two or more boards before you buy it.

The Ping-Pong Ball

This is a relatively inexpensive and yet incredibly effective training aid. Simply attach one end of a piece of string to a ping-pong or table-tennis ball and attach the other end to a ceiling or similar platform and you have a great training aid to help you develop your targeting. Although it can be used for developing many different techniques, this training aid is particularly useful for developing multiple kicks, as well as jumping kicks and jumping

spinning kicks. The length of the string can be varied according to the technique and target area you are training and, as your ability improves, particularly with the kicking drills, the string can be shortened to ensure your flexibility and jumping ability gets continuously pushed to its maximum.

Non-Contact Sparring

Admittedly, for this type of training you will need a partner to work with, although it doesn't necessarily have to be someone that understands kickboxing to the same level as yourself. Sparring is quite simply the process of fighting in a controlled manner. There are many forms of sparring that you can practise, ranging from non-contact, where no contact is made at all, to semi-contact, where the power exerted is reduced so the actual amount of contact made is a lot less than it could be in a real life situation, to full contact, where the power exerted is a hard as the fighter can deliver. The type of sparring that is used in kickboxing will vary depending on the rules that the particular style adheres to, and it is not uncommon for kickboxing to fall into either the semi-contact or full-contact sector.

Non-contact sparring is generally the chosen method when first starting out, as it allows both fighters to spar in the same way as if contact had been introduced, but reduces the risk of either fighter getting injured. There are many different ways that non-contact sparring can be done and below are some of the training methods that can be used:

- One person attacks only using a set technique (for example, just using a jab) and the other person simulates the appropriate defences for that technique. Ensure the techniques fall short of the training partner and vary the time from one-minute to three-minute rounds.
- One person attacks, using multiple techniques (either punches, kicks or both) and the other person defends accordingly. Follow the same guidelines as above.
- Both attack and defend at the same time, aiming at any gaps in the defences of the opponent but again without actual contact. Simulate defending the attacks as you see them and isolate punches, kicks and individual techniques, as well as free play (anything goes).

9 Jumping Kicks

We now start to venture into the advanced kicking stage of the book and this chapter focuses on the jumping kick. As you will be starting to understand by now, the kicks within kickboxing all take on the same theme. The difference is how they are performed. For example, the front kick can be performed off either leg, with or without a jump and with or without a spin. The same can be said for the round kick, the side kick and, in fact, all of the static kicks contained within a kickboxing syllabus. As we progress through this chapter you will discover how to take each of the static kicks and turn them into a jumping kick. This will then give you the distinct advantage of being able to perform each kick from standing, spinning, jumping and even jumping spinning.

Be aware that jumping kicks are quite exhausting to perform, which is why you don't generally see them done as much as the static kicks within a competitive environment. They can also leave you quite vulnerable to attack due to the fact that you bring both feet off the floor at some point and there is normally some kind of pre-movement prior to the jump taking place, which helps to prepare you for the spring and generate the energy that is needed to get off the floor. Saying that though, they can be extremely powerful and when you incorporate a spin into the jump, as you will see in the next chapter, then they become quite devastating.

Basic Jumping Kicks

There are two ways with which to perform a jumping kick, namely: a bicycle-action jump, aptly named due to the peddling motion used to jump into the air; or a straight jump, also known as the pop-up, which incorporates a vertical jump straight up with both feet leaving the ground at the same time. Within these two variations of jump there is also the ability to perform the kick off either the front leg or the rear leg. Therefore, you actually have a total of four different ways with which to perform each jumping kick, and this is excluding whether you jump for height or jump for distance. If this is all a little confusing to begin with, then read on and everything will become clear.

Let's start at the very beginning with the jumping front kick. For ease of understanding we'll stick to the same formula for each type of kick and work through the various different versions in the same order. We'll also now incorporate a training partner, holding a mix of focus pads, to demonstrate how the kick can be used for height; also holding a kick shield, to show how the kick can be used for either distance, power or both. As you train these kicks, try mixing them up so that you develop height, distance and power; use the correct training aid and appropriate training method to develop each kick correctly, as shown in the demonstrations. You may also want to refer back to the chapter on static kicks (*see* Chapter 6) to check striking parts and detailed movements if necessary.

The Jumping Front Kick – Lead Leg Using Bicycle-Action Jump for Height

In a front stance (Figure 310), bring your back leg straight up in a vertical motion, as high as you can (Figure 311). As your rear leg reaches its maximum height, use the energy of this movement to spring into the air off your other leg (Figure 312). As you start to increase in height, switch the legs in mid-air (Figure 313) and drive the lead leg upwards towards the target, while the other leg begins its descent in readiness for your landing (Figure 314).

Fig 310 In a front stance …

Fig 311 … bring your rear leg up with momentum.

Fig 312 Jump off your stationary leg.

Fig 313 Switch the legs in mid-air.

Fig 314 Drive the kicking leg upwards towards the target.

The Jumping Front Kick – Rear Leg Using Bicycle-Action Jump for Distance

Now stand a little further away from the target but still working from a front stance (Figure 315). Transfer your body weight on to your rear leg, so that this time you can bring your lead leg up high into the air to start the kick (Figure 316). You may have to adjust the length of your stance slightly in order to achieve this, as a long stance will prevent you from lifting the leg off the floor and cause you to step up, which will slow the kick down further and telegraph the technique. Ideally, for this you want your rear leg positioned just underneath your body (as shown in Figure 315). Using the energy of this motion, spring off your rear leg, propelling the body forwards and towards the target (Figure 317). Switch the legs in mid-air, driving the kicking leg through to the front (Figure 318) and strike the target with the correct part of the foot (Figure 319).

The last two kicks used the bicycle-action jump to assist the take-off and we looked at gaining height with the first one and distance with the second. This was done to enable you to understand the action required for these two different energies and that there is no set rule for how this can be done. Either of the kicks could be used for

Fig 315 At a distance and in a front stance ...

Fig 316 ... bring your lead leg into the air.

Fig 317 Jump off your rear leg.

Fig 318 Switch the legs in mid-air.

Fig 319 Strike the target correctly.

height or for distance, and the rear leg is just as effective when used to achieve height with a kick, in the same way as the lead leg can be used to cover distance.

The parameters that determine which kick is used in which situation is simply down to your body position, your weight distribution prior to take-off, the position of the target and, of course, timing. The skill is in determining, in an instant, which process is the most effective in the allocated time you have with which to perform the kick, based on how you are standing and where your target is positioned. In time, this process becomes instantaneous and your ability to react will take place without conscious thought. However, this skill doesn't come for free and certainly isn't an overnight development, but it does come eventually through training. Before moving on any further, try training these two kicks thoroughly, so that you fully understand the jumping motion required to perform them correctly. Take each kick in turn and, ideally using a punchbag or training partner holding pads, train for both height and distance off both sides.

**The Jumping Front Kick – Lead Leg
Using Straight Jump for Height**

In a front stance, stand with your lead leg positioned close to, if not directly underneath, your body (Figure 320). Bend the legs slightly in order to prepare for the jump and assist with the spring (Figure 321). Jump into the air (Figure 322) and, at the same time, bring the knees up as high as you can (Figure 323). As you reach your highest point, extend the kicking leg out towards the target, striking with the correct part of the foot and tucking the rear leg up at the same time (Figure 324).

In order for this kick to go through the proper motions, your pad holder needs to ensure the target is held correctly. The temptation for an inexperienced pad holder is to hold the focus pad so that the kicking area is parallel to the floor. Take care to ensure that this is not the case, as it is a common occurrence and will give you a false kicking target. Rarely will you kick anything at this height in that position; this bad practice also forces you to kick with the instep instead of the ball of the foot, which is of course wrong and quite dangerous, as it can

Fig 320 In a front stance ...

Fig 321 ... bend the knees to prepare
for the jump.

Fig 322 Jump into the air, bringing
both feet off the floor together.

Fig 323 Bring the knees up high.

Fig 324 Strike the target with the correct part of the foot.

Fig 325 In a front stance, stand at a distance from your target.

result in broken toes or, worse, a broken foot. Instead, ensure the pad is held at a slight angle, as shown, as this gives a more realistic target and ensures the correct striking part of the foot is used.

The Jumping Front Kick – Rear Leg Using Straight Jump for Distance

In a front stance, stand at a distance from your target (Figure 325). Bend the knees once more to prepare for the jump (Figure 326). As you jump into the air this time, project your body forwards, so you start to travel towards the target (Figure 327). Switch your legs in mid-air (Figure 328) and, as you near the target, drive the rear leg through to connect with the correct striking part of the foot (Figure 329).

As with the previous two kicks, train these last two thoroughly before moving any further and ensure you capture each stage of this new jumping process correctly. The method for both the bicycle-action jump and the straight jump is fairly standard for all the kicks that follow, so a good understanding now will make the rest of this section easier to follow. The only difference from here on is the

Fig 326 Bend the knees to prepare for the jump.

Fig 327 Jump towards your target.

Fig 328 Switch the legs in mid-air.

Fig 329 Strike the target correctly.

change of body mechanics that are required, in order to ensure the different kicks land correctly, based on the way the kick is designed to travel.

Try working the lead leg for height and distance to start with and then follow with the rear leg for height and distance as well. This will help you to understand the process required for both types of jump, using either the rear or the lead leg, and covering either height or distance or even both.

The Jumping Round Kick – Lead Leg Using Bicycle Action

When working the round kick as a static style kick, an angular stance is generally more effective as a starting point because the leg is already in the best position for the kick. This also ensures the time taken for the kick to travel from its starting point to the target is as fast as possible and eliminates any unnecessary movement that would otherwise be required if more of a front stance was used.

Where the jumping kicks are concerned, however, this little rule changes, as anything other than a front stance can sometimes hinder the kick due to the lead leg obstructing the rear leg for the take-off process. That's not to say that a jumping kick can't be performed from an angular or side stance, it's just that when you first start out learning this kick, it may be easier to begin in a front stance, as to start out in any other stance requires a little more understanding of movement and body mechanics, and may be a little too much to grasp at such an early stage.

From a front stance (Figure 330), bring the rear leg up as high as you can (Figure 331). As the knee reaches the highest point, use the energy of this motion to jump off the lead leg (Figure 332). As you start to gain height, twist the body in mid-air by driving the kicking leg round in a circular motion (Figure 333) and drive the leg towards the target, striking with the correct part of the foot (Figure 334).

The twisting motion of this kick will make it a little trickier to master compared with the jumping front kick; however, practise, practise, practise and you will eventually get it. Be sure to keep your guard tight on all the jumping kicks to ensure you are covered throughout the full range of movement, and particularly on landing. You may also

find that the trend with the bicycle-action kicks is that the rear non-kicking leg can sometimes straighten out once the kick connects. This is nothing to worry about and for some kicks is quite natural. The advantage that this can also have is when it comes to the landing, as your non-kicking leg is already there to support you on your descent.

The Jumping Round Kick – Rear Leg Using Bicycle Action

From a front stance (Figure 335), transfer your body weight on to your rear leg and bring your lead leg high into the air (Figure 336). As you do, use the energy of this motion to jump off your rear leg (Figure 337) and switch the legs in mid-air as you gain height (Figure 338). From here, start twisting the body to prepare for the kick (Figure 339) and, finally, drive the kicking leg through in a circular motion, striking the target with the correct part of the foot (Figure 340).

Fig 330 From a front stance …

Fig 331 ... drive your rear leg up high.

Fig 332 Jump off the lead leg.

Fig 333 Twist the body in mid-air.

Fig 334 Drive the leg in a circular motion towards the target.

Fig 335 From a front stance ...

Fig 336 ... bring your lead leg up high.

Fig 337 Jump off the rear leg.

Fig 338 Switch the legs in mid-air.

Fig 339 Start driving the kick round in a circular motion.

Fig 340 Kick the target with the correct striking part of the foot.

The Jumping Round Kick – Lead Leg Using Straight Jump

From an angled stance (Figure 341), bend the knees to prepare for the jump (Figure 342). Spring up as high as you can, bringing both feet off the floor at the same time (Figure 343), and bring the knees up high, chambering the leg in preparation for the kick (Figure 344). From this position start extending the lead leg out using a circular motion (Figure 345) and, as you reach your highest point, drive the leg through, connecting with the target using the correct striking part of the foot (Figure 346).

The Jumping Round Kick – Rear Leg Using Straight Jump

From a front-on or angled stance (Figure 347), bend the knees in preparation for the jump (Figure 348). Jump as high in the air as you can and bring both feet off the floor at the same time (Figure 349). Bring the knees up high and, as you gain height, start twisting the body round in a circular motion, so that the rear leg starts its journey

towards the target (Figure 350). As the body comes round, drive the kicking leg through to strike the target with the correct part of the foot (Figure 351).

With these two versions of the jumping round kick, the legs, or rather the knees, remain up high as the kick connects. This is different in practice to the bicycle-action jumping motion and also helps to protect the groin area when in mid-flight. Unlike the bicycle-action jump, where the rear leg is positioned a little straighter and assists with the landing, the feet travelling together with the straight jump is of no real hindrance to the kick and, as you will discover from practice, assists with the landing just as well. This completes the jumping round kick using both jumping techniques and kicking off both the rear and lead leg. It is the first of the circular jumping kicks and if you can master this one it will set you up nicely for the jumping kicks that follow. One tip to consider from this point on is, if possible, train the jumping kicks and the jumping spinning kicks on a matted surface just in case you miss your landing.

Fig 341 From an angled stance …

Fig 342 … bend the knees to prepare for the jump.

Fig 343 Jump as high as you can with both feet.

Fig 344 Bring the knees up high.

Fig 345 Start driving the kick round in a circular motion.

Fig 346 Execute the kick.

Fig 347 From a front-on stance …

Fig 348 … bend the knees to start the jump.

Fig 349 Jump as high as possible.

Fig 350 Bring the knees up and start
the twisting motion.

Fig 351 Drive the leg through towards
the target.

The Jumping Side Kick – Lead Leg Using Bicycle Action

The jumping side kick uses a very similar motion
of travel to the jumping round kick, so if you
found the last one relatively easy to grasp, then
this one should be of no real problem for you. You
may also notice that the bicycle-action jump for
this kick also allows the non-kicking leg to hang
down, whereas the straight-jump version enables
you to bring your non-kicking leg up to protect
the groin area. This will also allow you to stay in
the air longer and, by using forward motion, travel over obstacles with relative ease.

A little-known fact is that the jumping side kick
was originally developed many years ago for the
battlefield and is designed to kick an enemy off a
horse. The process of covering the groin with the
rear foot was done to clear the horse and also to
protect this vital area from attack with a sword, or
similar weapon, at the same time. In this day and
age, the need to kick people off horses isn't as
common; however, the kick still remains true to its
roots and you may well find in tournaments up

and down the country, that there are still tae kwon do practitioners jumping huge distances to break blocks of wood, using this particular style of kick.

From your front-on stance (Figure 352), bring the rear leg up as high as possible to add energy to the take off (Figure 353). As the knee reaches its highest point, use the energy of this movement to spring off the lead leg (Figure 354). As the kicking leg comes off the floor, twist the body to bring the lead leg in line with the target (Figure 355) and, when the knee of the kicking leg passes the centre line, thrust the kick out in a straight line and strike the target with the correct part of the foot (Figure 356).

Fig 352 From a front stance …

Fig 353 … bring the rear leg up high.

Fig 354 Jump off the lead leg.

Fig 355 Twist the body while in the air.

Fig 356 Stab the leg out in a straight line towards the target.

The Jumping Side Kick – Rear Leg Using Bicycle Action

From a front stance (Figure 357), transfer your weight to the rear leg, allowing you to bring the lead leg off the floor (Figure 358). As you do, use the energy of this motion to spring up off your rear leg (Figure 359). Bring the rear leg up as high as possible and, at the same time, use the momentum of this manoeuvre to turn the body side-on while in the air (Figure 360). As the knee of the kicking leg passes the centre line, drive the kick out in a perfectly straight line towards the target and straighten the rear leg at the same time to prepare for the landing (Figure 361).

Fig 357 From a front stance …

Fig 358 … bring the lead leg off the floor.

Fig 359 Jump off your rear leg.

Fig 360 Twist the body in the air.

Fig 361 Kick the target correctly.

The Jumping Side Kick – Lead Leg
Using Straight Jump

This particular jumping side kick should be the easiest of all the four versions to perform. To assist with this we are going to work off more of a side stance, due to the way the kick works in practice. It can be done from an angular stance or even a front-on stance; however, for speed and ease of understanding, try working off a side stance to begin with. Once you have mastered this approach, try varying the stances to give you a different experience.

This time, from a side-on stance (Figure 362), bend the knees to prepare for the jump (Figure 363). Spring up as high as you can (Figure 364) and tuck the knees into the body at the same time (Figure 365). When the jump reaches its highest point, shoot the kick out in a straight line and strike the target with the correct part of the foot (Figure 366).

Fig 362 From a side stance ...

Fig 363 ... bend the knees to prepare for the jump.

Fig 364 Spring up as high as you can.

Fig 365 Tuck the knees up high.

Fig 366 Kick the target correctly.

**The Jumping Side Kick – Rear Leg
Using Straight Jump**

In contrast to the last kick, this one may possibly be the hardest of the four jumping side kicks to master and you may well benefit from a little more time spent practising this one. As the motion for this kick involves a near 180-degree rotation of the body, it would be advisable to start off in a front stance in order to reduce that extra movement a little more. This will also speed up the kick and make it easier to transition from the start position to the end position.

By now you should be fairly competent with the stances and, although each kick has its advisory stance, it is just that – advisory. To have the ability to perform every kick from every stance and every position is the dream of most martial artists, so feel free to play around a little with the stances and, if you feel ready, play around with the breakdown of each of the kicks as well, until you find a method of application that works better for you.

Most instructors will teach you the way it works best for them. Your job is then to take that information and adapt it so that it works best for you, while still achieving the same end result. This could also be one of the reasons why a lot of martial arts students fail to achieve an acceptable ability level for their grade. The unfortunate truth is 'if the instructor can't do it, they don't show their students'.

From a front stance (Figure 367), bend the knees once more to prepare you for the jump (Figure 368). From this position, jump as high as you can into the air, bringing your knees up high at the same time (Figure 369). As you travel upwards, start twisting the body to begin the process of bringing your kicking leg through to the front (Figure 370). As your kicking leg passes the centre line, drive the kick out in a perfectly straight line and use the energy of the twisting motion to generate additional power for the kick, while bringing the rear leg up to protect the groin at the same time (Figure 371).

Fig 367 From a front stance …

Fig 368 … bend the knees to prepare for the jump.

Fig 369 Jump as high as you can.

Fig 370 Twist the body to bring the kicking leg to the front.

Fig 371 Kick the target with the correct striking part.

The Jumping Hook Kick – Lead Leg Using Bicycle Action

Of all the jumping kicks available to the kickboxer, this set is possibly the most difficult to grasp, due to the way the leg travels prior to the kick landing. For the beginner, the static hooking kick is a difficult kick to learn and, when a jump is added to it, the kick becomes one that could quite easily be missed out of a training programme, as previously mentioned (*if the instructor can't do it, they don't show their students*). For that reason, I would advise you to persevere with this kick, despite what your head may be telling you to do, especially as perseverance is one of the key attributes to a good martial arts student. Plus, the extra effort put in here will reap huge rewards for you in the future, in more ways than one.

From a front stance (Figure 372), bring the rear leg up as high as you can (Figure 373). Use the energy of this motion to jump off the lead leg (Figure 374). Twist the body as you travel through the air, driving the kicking leg past the target (Figure 375). As the foot passes the target (almost as if you are executing a side kick that misses its mark), whip the leg back in and strike using either the heel or the ball of the foot (Figure 376).

Fig 372 From a front stance ...

Fig 373 ... bring the rear leg up high.

Fig 374 Jump off the lead leg.

Fig 375 Drive the kicking leg past the target by twisting the body.

Fig 376 Whip the leg back to connect with the heel or the ball of the foot.

The Jumping Hook Kick – Rear Leg Using Bicycle Action

From a front-on stance (Figure 377), bring your lead leg up as high as you can (Figure 378). Jump off the rear leg (Figure 379) and, as you do, drive the rear kicking leg through to the front (Figure 380). Twist the body to turn yourself side-on and drive the leg past the target at the same time (Figure 381). Then hook the leg back in towards the target and strike with the correct part of the foot (Figure 382).

The Jumping Hook Kick – Lead Leg Using Straight Jump

The jumping hook kick is very similar in motion to the jumping side kick. The only real difference is the hooking motion of the leg at the end of the kick that is used to perform the strike. For that reason, if at this stage you can perform a jumping side kick relatively well, then the jumping hook kick shouldn't be that much more difficult. On that note, this particular version of the jumping hook kick might be best performed off a side-on stance, in the same way as the equivalent jumping side kick was earlier in the chapter.

Fig 377 From a front stance ...

Fig 378 ... bring your lead leg up high.

Fig 379 Jump off the rear leg.

Fig 380 Twist the body to turn side-on.

Fig 381 Extend the kicking leg past the target.

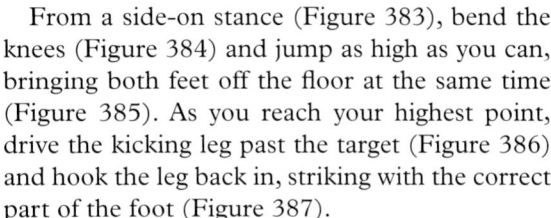

From a side-on stance (Figure 383), bend the knees (Figure 384) and jump as high as you can, bringing both feet off the floor at the same time (Figure 385). As you reach your highest point, drive the kicking leg past the target (Figure 386) and hook the leg back in, striking with the correct part of the foot (Figure 387).

The Jumping Hook Kick – Rear Leg Using Straight Jump

I would say that this version of the jumping hook kick is possibly the hardest one and coincidentally it is the very last one we look at before we change kicks. Due to the way the body and the kick need to work against one another, it may well be the one you struggle with. From a front-on stance (Figure 388), jump as high as you can, bringing both feet into the air at the same time (Figure 389). As you gain height, start to twist the body to get position and drive your kicking leg through to the front (Figure 390). Extend the kicking leg out past the target (Figure 391), and hook the leg back in again striking with the correct part of the foot (Figure 392).

Fig 382 Hook the leg back in to attack.

Fig 383 From a side-on stance ...

Fig 384 ... bend the knees.

Fig 385 Jump as high as you can.

Fig 386 Drive the kicking leg out past the target.

Fig 387 Hook the kick back in, striking with the correct part of the foot.

Fig 388 From a front stance …

Fig 389 … jump into air, bringing both feet up at the same time.

Fig 390 Twist the body.

Fig 391 Extend the kick out past the target.

Fig 392 Hook the leg back in again.

The Jumping Axe Kick – Lead Leg
Using Bicycle Action

As with the static axe kick, the jumping version has the same rules and works in much the same way. Designed to attack the blind side of an opponent, the kick is most effective when it travels across your body, adding that extra level of cover and protection when you are in mid-jump. The area to be particularly careful with for this kick is the landing, as you do end up quite close to the opponent once the kick has done its job. A simple adjustment of the body position, however, can keep the vital areas covered or out of danger completely and should ensure you are not left open to a possible counter-strike.

From your front-on position in a left lead, and with your partner also standing in a left lead (Figure 393), bring the rear leg up as high as you can (Figure 394). Using this motion to generate the energy needed for the jump, spring off your left leg (Figure 395) and take the kick across your body,

so that it travels from the start position to the outside of the opponent's lead shoulder (providing they have their left side in front) in an anti-clockwise motion (Figure 396). As the knee passes the opponent's blind shoulder, straighten the leg (Figure 397) and drive the kick in a downwards motion aiming for either the top of the head or the side of the face, depending on the reaction of the opponent at this point (Figure 398). Finally, land the leg with control, keeping the guard up and the body and head slightly back and out of the reach of a possible counter-strike (Figure 399).

The Jumping Axe Kick – Rear Leg
Using Bicycle Action

The rear leg jumping axe kick is used to attack an opponent that has an opposite stance to you, for example your left leg forwards and their right leg forwards. This now gives you the ability to use a jumping axe kick and attack across the blind shoulder of an opponent, regardless of which leg they

Fig 393 From a front stance in a left lead ...

Fig 394 ... bring the rear leg up high.

Fig 395 Jump off the left leg.

Fig 396 Bring the leg up using an anti-clockwise motion.

Fig 397 Straighten the leg out fully.

Fig 398 Drive the kick down towards the target.

Fig 399 Land correctly, keeping yourself protected.

have in front. It also allows you to attack the blind side of an opponent regardless of which leg you have in front, which works particularly well if you find yourself in the wrong stance for whatever reason.

From a front stance in a left lead, but with your partner standing in a right lead (Figure 400), bring your lead leg up as high as you can (Figure 401). Use the energy of this movement to jump off your rear leg (Figure 402) and drive the kick towards the blind side of your opponent using a clockwise motion (Figure 403). As the kick passes over their shoulder, straighten the leg (Figure 404) and drive the kick down to strike the target, using the correct part of the foot (Figure 405).

The Jumping Axe Kick – Lead Leg Using Straight Jump

You may well find this version the most awkward of the jumping styles to perform using an axe kick, due to the way the legs move naturally and the ease of the bicycle-jump motion based on this natural movement. Despite this it is certainly worth understanding this kick and a little time and practice spent on this particular technique will certainly pay off at some point in the future, if you are serious about your martial arts.

Working from a front stance in a left lead, with your partner in a left lead also (Figure 406), bend your knees in preparation for the jump (Figure 407). Spring up as high as you can (Figure 408) and, when you reach your maximum height, straighten out the leg, bringing it over the opponent's blind shoulder (Figure 409) and drive it straight down on to the target, attacking with the correct part of the foot (Figure 410) and landing correctly (Figure 411).

The Jumping Axe Kick – Rear Leg Using Straight Jump

Working from a front stance in a left lead, with your partner in a right lead (Figure 412), bend the knees slightly to prepare for the jump (Figure 413).

Fig 400 In a front stance ...

Fig 401 ... bring the lead leg up.

Fig 402 Jump off the rear leg.

Fig 403 Drive the kick round in a clockwise motion.

Fig 404 Straighten the leg in preparation for the kick.

Fig 405 Strike the target using the correct part of the foot.

Fig 406 In a front stance ...

Fig 407 ... bend your knees.

Fig 408 Jump up as high as you can, driving the kicking leg forwards.

Fig 409 Straighten out the leg.

Fig 410 Drive the kick down on to the target.

Fig 411 Landing correctly afterwards.

Fig 412 In a front stance …

Fig 413 … bend the knees to prepare for the jump.

Fig 414 Jump into the air off both feet.

Fig 415 Switch legs in mid-air, driving the kicking leg through.

Fig 416 Straighten the kicking leg out.

Fig 417 Drive the kick down on to the target.

Fig 418 In a front stance ...

Fig 419 ... bring the rear leg up high.

Spring up as high as you can, bringing both feet off the floor at the same time, and tuck the knees up towards the body as you do so (Figure 414). Drive your kicking leg forwards and switch your legs while in mid-air (Figure 415). When the forward leg passes over the blind shoulder of your opponent, straighten the leg (Figure 416) and drive the kick down on to the target (Figure 417).

The Jumping Outside Crescent Kick – Lead Leg Using Bicycle Action
As mentioned in the chapter on static kicks, the crescent kick is an incredibly versatile kick that can be used in a variety of distances, including very close range. The jumping version takes the kick to the next stage and can generate an incredible amount of power, when performed correctly. As such, the outside crescent kick is a very effective technique that can be used for both offensive and defensive reaction, and the ability to strike with either the inside or the outside of the foot makes this kick one of the most adaptable kicks within kickboxing.

Due to the forward position of the body when striking with this kick, a front-on stance is probably the more effective starting point with which to begin and, for ease of understanding, we'll start in a left lead (Figure 418). From here bring the rear knee up as high as you can to start the jumping process (Figure 419). Jump off the kicking leg in the normal way (Figure 420) and, as you do, bring the same leg across your body as you did for the jumping axe kick but this time take the kick around in a semicircular motion, travelling in an anti-clockwise direction (Figure 421). As the leg lines up with the target, drive the kick back in towards its mark, striking with the outside of the foot (Figure 422). You will note that with this kick, the supporting leg may well hang down as you jump into the air. As with all the bicycle-action jumps, this is perfectly normal and will assist you again with the landing. You can also choose to attack over the blind side of your opponent or attack to the open side. Just be aware that, due to the direction of travel with a crescent kick, you may need a reasonable level of flexibility to achieve a head-height strike, if you go for the blind side; otherwise may find yourself striking the lead shoulder of your opponent, which will, of course, result in a loss of overall effect.

Fig 420 Jump off the kicking leg.

Fig 421 Drive the kicking leg around in an anti-clockwise motion.

Fig 422 Kick the target with the correct part of the foot, using a crescent motion.

The Jumping Outside Crescent Kick – Rear Leg Using Bicycle Action

The rear-leg version of this jumping kick will allow you to respond very quickly with an attack or counter, without the need to ensure your opponent is in the correct position, i.e. blind side forwards. This kick, combined with the last one, will allow you to incorporate a jumping outside crescent kick into your attack, regardless of which leg you or your opponent has in front.

From a left lead in a front stance (Figure 423), bring the lead leg up as high as you can to prepare for the jump (Figure 424). Use the ballistic energy of this movement to jump off the rear, kicking leg (Figure 425), switching the legs in mid-air and bringing your kicking leg across your body in a clockwise motion, keeping it slightly bent as it travels (Figure 426). From here, use the hips and body to drive the leg back in towards the target in a crescent motion and strike with a straight leg, using the correct part of the foot (Figure 427).

The whipping motion as demonstrated with this kick is of the utmost importance should you wish to generate any real power from an outside

Fig 423 In a front stance ...

Fig 424 … bring the lead leg up as high as you can.

Fig 425 Jump off the rear leg.

Fig 426 Switch the legs in mid-air.

Fig 427 Drive the leg back towards the target, using a crescent motion.

crescent kick. It can be done by just swinging the leg in a crescent fashion and, in its defence, this particular method of execution may well generate some additional energy. However, in order to get the maximum out of the kick and use it with the greatest effect, try to incorporate this whipping motion by keeping the leg bent until the last

Fig 428 In a front stance ...

Fig 429 ... prepare for the jump.

minute and see what happens. This manoeuvre may require a bit more training but, once you can get it to work, makes a massive difference to the overall power of the kick.

The Jumping Outside Crescent Kick – Lead Leg Using Straight Jump

The straight jump that this technique focuses on offers a little more speed, allowing for a slightly faster attack or counter-attack, particularly when using it off the rear leg. The straight jump motion probably doesn't complement the lead-leg version of this technique as much as it does the rear leg and, as with the inside crescent kick (to follow), you may have a higher success rate with this kick if targeting the open side of the opponent's body, as opposed to the blind side.

From a front stance in a left lead (Figure 428), bend the legs slightly to prepare for the jump (Figure 429). Spring into the air as high as you can, and tuck your legs up into the body as you do (Figure 430). Bring the lead leg out and across the body in an anticlockwise motion, in preparation for the kick (Figure 431), and whip the leg back in again towards the target and connect with the correct part of the foot (Figure 432).

Fig 430 Jump as high as you can.

Fig 431 Start the kick travelling in a circular motion.

Fig 432 Strike the target, using the correct part of the foot.

The Jumping Outside Crescent Kick – Rear Leg Using Straight Jump

The final kick in the jumping outside crescent kick category probably finishes with one of the most fun kicks of all the jumping kicks covered so far. The straight jump motion works well with this kick and, with a little time and training, can not only help to make the kick incredibly quick, but also extremely powerful.

From a front-on stance in a left lead (Figure 433), using the same motion as before to prepare for the take off (Figure 434), jump into the air with both feet leaving the ground at the same time (Figure 435). As you start to gain height twist the body, driving the kicking leg through to the front, enabling the legs to switch positions by the time you have reached the peak of the jump (Figure 436). As the front leg lines up with the target, drive the kick back in, using the body, and allow the leg to straighten naturally, striking the target with the outside of the foot, as before (Figure 437).

The Jumping Inside Crescent Kick – Lead Leg Using Bicycle Action

This particular kick can be very effective as a set up for another technique, by using it at a distance to clear your opponent's guard out of the way. It also works slightly better if used to attack the open side of the opponent's body, as the lead shoulder of the closed or blind side can sometimes be a natural barrier against a kick of this nature, especially

Fig 433 From a front stance in a left lead ...

Fig 434 ... bend the legs slightly.

Fig 435 Jump high into the air.

Fig 436 Switch the legs when in mid-air.

Fig 437 Strike the target with the correct part of the foot.

Fig 438 From a front stance ...

Fig 439 ... drive your rear leg up.

crescent kick is to let the leg land naturally and then recover, instead of trying to manipulate the leg back into its original position and finding yourself off balance or vulnerable to a counter-attack, due to the focus on trying to control the landing.

Think of this kick as being more of an explosive technique and this may help you to understand that, in order to get the maximum energy behind it, you simply need to let the kick go and allow the leg to land where it wants to land. Therefore, when practising, put some time into the landing and recovery, as well as the trajectory, and you may find that this potentially awkward kick could become one of your best weapons.

From a left lead front-on stance, with your partner also in a left lead front-on stance (Figure 438), drive the rear leg up to generate the energy for the jump (Figure 439). As the rear leg reaches its highest point, jump off your lead leg (Figure 440) and drive your kicking leg through to the front, in a semicircular clockwise motion, to the open side of your opponent (Figure 441). As the kick reaches its peak, straighten the leg and drive the kick in towards the target striking with the correct part of the foot (Figure 442).

due to the fact that it travels in a horizontal style crescent motion, as opposed to the vertical movement associated with the axe kick, for example.

Inexperienced students tend to struggle a little with this kick, due to the way the leg wants to land after the kick has been executed (providing the foot hasn't bounced back off the target, of course). The simplest way of advancing from a jumping inside

Fig 440 Jump off your lead leg.

Fig 441 Drive your kicking leg towards your opponent.

Fig 442 Strike with the correct part of the foot.

The Jumping Inside Crescent Kick –
Rear Leg Using Bicycle Action

This version of the kick is a very effective way of attacking the open side of your opponent, if they either switch to an opposite lead or prefer to fight off a different side to you. It can be performed with incredible speed, due to the lack of complexity involved in the movements. Due to the energy generated from the jump, it is likely to penetrate the toughest of guards in order to find its mark. As it is also an effective close-range kick, it is very versatile and can be used with confidence from almost any range. The only word of warning with this kick is to be wary of your opponent counterattacking, as you can find yourself quite vulnerable and off-balance, if not careful.

From a left lead front stance, with your partner in a right lead front stance (Figure 443), drive your lead leg up as high as possible (Figure 444). Once this leg reaches its highest point, jump off the back leg and start to chamber the kick (Figure 445). Start extending the kicking leg and let the energy of this motion drive the kick towards the target, travelling in an anticlockwise direction (Figure 446) and land the leg naturally keeping your guard tight (Figure 447).

Fig 443 In a front stance ...

Fig 444 ... bring the lead leg up high.

The Jumping Inside Crescent Kick –
Lead Leg Using Straight Jump

This kick may be the most awkward of the jumping inside crescent kick range, as it can be difficult to generate large amounts of power with this kick without over extending the kicking leg.

Fig 445 Jump off the rear leg.

Fig 446 Drive the kick in towards the target.

Fig 447 Land correctly.

Fig 448 In a front stance ...   Fig 449 ... bend the knees.   Fig 450 Jump off both feet.

Against an inexperienced opponent, this extra addition to the kick may well go unpunished; however, when faced with an experienced opponent, the additional step required to generate that extra bit of power may not go unnoticed and may result in a counter-strike before the kick has time to land. Spend some time on this one until you feel you are able to strike with a reasonable amount of energy, using as little telegraphing as possible. It can also be a great counter-strike kick against an advancing opponent but you will have to spend a little time on the explosive speed and timing in order to pull this one off.

In a left lead front stance, with your partner also in a left lead front stance (Figure 448), slightly bend the knees in preparation for the jump (Figure

Fig 451 Straighten out the leg.   Fig 452 Drive the kick back in towards the target.   Fig 453 Land correctly.

449). From this position, spring up into the air with both feet leaving the ground at the same time and at this point, start chambering the leg in readiness for the kick (Figure 450). As the jump reaches its peak, straighten the leg (Figure 451) and drive the kick in towards the open side of your target, using a semicircular motion and striking with the inside part of the foot (Figure 452). Be sure to land correctly with your guard kept tight (Figure 453).

The Jumping Inside Crescent Kick – Rear Leg Using Straight Jump

The final kick in the jumping kick range is one of the most effective close-range jumping kicks, due to the speed of travel from the floor to the target. It is also a very effective head-height kick that works just as well to the body, although you rarely see this kick used to target this area in competition. With some time spent on developing your timing, this kick can become a great defensive technique, as well as a very effective kick when used offensively.

In a left lead front stance, with your partner in a right lead front stance (Figure 454), bend the knees in readiness for the jump (Figure 455). Spring into the air as high as you can, bringing both feet off the floor at the same time and, as you do, start driving the rear leg in towards your opponent (Figure

Fig 454 From front-on stance in a left lead ...

Fig 455 ... bend the knees slightly to prepare for the jump.

456). As your leg lines up with your target, straighten it and drive it through, striking with the inside part of the foot (Figure 457), and land the leg naturally, keeping your guard tight at all times (Figure 458).

Fig 456 Spring into the air, bringing both feet of the floor at the same time.

Fig 457 Drive the kick in towards the target.

Fig 458 Land correctly.

Training Drills

By now you will be familiar with all the various ways with which to train the techniques and drills covered so far in the book. From here it is a simple case of varying the training methods to ensure that you are training each technique, in order to get the best out of it and to prevent the risk of boredom from setting in, which can happen if you are training aimlessly and without an objective or specific goal in mind.

The various training methods covered so far will help you to develop each of the elements that make up a kick or a punch, such as technical perfection, targeting, speed, energy, power, footwork, understanding of distance and range, body mechanics, movement, timing and so on. In order for the individual technique to be successful, each specific part needs to be in place, and these areas can be isolated and worked individually in order to hone that specific part, allowing you to bring it all together when sparring or competing.

In order to develop your body mechanics and technical perfection, try using training aids such as the mirror and the video camera. Targeting can be developed using focus pads, smash boards and the ping-pong ball. Power can be developed using a punch bag (in particular a heavy bag) and kick shields. Footwork and movement for each technique can be developed using shadow sparring and non-contact sparring. Speed can be developed using focus pads with a partner or a punch bag if training alone. Ankle weights and wrist weights can also be used to develop speed by performing slow repetitions, causing the muscles to develop at a much faster rate in order to compensate for the extra work they have to do due to the extra resistance that is added.

Whichever training method you choose, based on the element or technique you are looking to develop, ensure the length of time you train for is directly proportional to the rest period you allow yourself, based on your ability. As a complete beginner to kickboxing, it would be advisable to start off with no more than one minute of exercise coupled with one minute of rest. If you feel that you have not fully recovered at the end of your rest period, then simply increase the time you rest until you are at a stage where you can continue and complete another round unhindered.

The more advanced student can increase their round time accordingly and reduce the rest period to ensure they are fully recovered prior to starting the next round but not allowing time to cool down. The general rule is: the fitter you are, the faster you will recover; so it is not uncommon for the beginner to recover at a much slower rate to that of an experienced student.

As your body improves its ability to recover, increase the length of each round and decrease the rest period, if necessary, to ensure you are constantly pushing yourself but not getting cold in-between rounds. Naturally, don't indulge in the common practice amongst beginners of pushing yourself too fast too soon, as this will inevitably have an adverse effect on your training, as well as your body, and is a practice that is likely to cause a serious injury, which in turn, will put you out of action for some considerable time, negating all the hard work you may have put in to date.

10 Jumping Spinning Kicks

The jumping spinning kicks are probably the most difficult of all the kicks to master and yet it is these kicks that look the most impressive in any kicking art. There was a time when the jumping spinning kick was only really found in Asian movies and only then was the full magnificence of the kick only encapsulated by martial artists doubling as actors, with the training and ability to pull them off.

In more recent times, the jumping spinning kicks have found their way into displays or demonstrations, as these, much like the movies, can be choreographed to not only make the kick as impressive as can possibly be achieved by the martial artist performing it, but also made to look effective at the same time. The latter point is a key topic for many a heated discussion among martial artists of varying styles today.

Arts such as tae kwon do introduced the jumping spinning kick to the masses on a more commercialized basis and, although the art can only show but the individual must be able to perform, this didn't stop the nation's desire to kick like the late great Bruce Lee, or, more recently perhaps, the movie star Jean Claude Van Damme (who really made the jumping spinning kick famous in the Western movie world) and ensured that kicking arts such as tae kwon do became a popular choice of martial art among the would-be kickers of the world and helped to establish this Korean art as a household name.

As time progressed and fantasy became reality, thanks to the popularity of events such as cage fighting and the various spin-offs this style of combative fighting has created, the kicking arts took a slight backseat, as the more competitive martial artists, who wanted to test their skills against a like-minded opponent in a more realistic setting, started to emerge. Training in more direct full contact, stand-up arts and a whole new era of ground-fighting started and, as the exponent skilled in the art of ground-fighting seemed to have the edge on the stand-up fighter, a new wave of training emerged.

As with all trends that come and go or, in this case, take their rightful place in the martial arts world, it can be seen that this new style of fighter paved the way for how martial arts are studied and taught today. Visit the vast majority of schools up and down the country and you will find that they are no longer specialists in one specific style but instead offer mixed styles to give the student the best of both worlds.

Just like with fashion that also comes and goes (and martial arts are certainly a fashionable thing to do for many), it can once again be seen that stand-up arts are starting to make a comeback. Spinning kicks, and, indeed, jumping spinning kicks, are beginning to appear in reality-style events, which just goes to show that, although a large consensus will happily discuss the ineffectiveness of the jumping spinning kick all day long, you only have to witness someone capable of pulling off a kick of this nature, to prove that, with a good understanding of range and timing combined with a lot of hard work and training, anything is possible.

Basic Jumping Spinning Kicks

Due to the complexity of the jumping spinning kick, this chapter has purposefully been left till now. If you have followed the book correctly, you should be confident enough to tackle this section with more competence than you would have had if you had simply turned to this section first. As mentioned in Chapter 4, the foundations are the most important part of studying any martial art and these are developed through repetition of basic techniques.

The student that understands this will go on to have a long and prosperous journey in the martial arts. However, the unfortunate truth is that in this modern-day world with which we live, things like fast food, the latest technology and the internet all help to develop this instantaneous 'everything now' attitude within us, and unfortunately this is not conducive to success in the martial arts. This attitude can be the downfall of the would-be martial artist, resulting in boredom and/or a lack of interest once the 'honeymoon' period (normally the first ninety days of starting a martial art) is over and subsequently resulting in the end of the study.

In order to be successful at anything, you need to understand that nothing is for free, just as nothing comes instantly. Your progress is the direct result of how hard you work and your success is the result of your perseverance, persistence and commitment and the absolute refusal to quit, regardless of how hard (or boring) something may be. Invest some time in your basics, which will in turn build the foundations you need to make you a better and all-rounded martial artist. Only then will you be able to perform advanced techniques, such as jumping spinning kicks and the like, with relative ease and effort and, in turn, help to make this part of your study much more successful and enjoyable.

The Jumping Spinning Front Kick

Despite the name 'jumping spinning kick' not all of these kicks involve a true spin. Some involve more of a twisting motion and the jumping spinning front kick is the first of these twisting-style spinning kicks. Read the breakdown very carefully to ensure you are moving through each stage of the kick correctly, otherwise you may well find that the end result of this kick may not be quite the same is it should be.

From a slightly angled stance in a left lead (Figure 459), start twisting your body backwards in a clockwise motion, looking over your right shoulder to spot the opponent. Note how the front foot pivots to set the body up for the spin (Figure 460). At this point, start bringing your rear (right) leg up into the air (Figure 461). Using the energy of the spin, jump off your left leg

Fig 459 In a left lead working from an angled stance ...

Fig 460 ... twist your body round in a clockwise motion.

Fig 461 Bring the non-kicking leg off the floor.

Fig 462 Jump off your kicking leg.

Fig 463 Twist the body round towards your target.

(Figure 462) and continue to drive the body round towards the target (Figure 463). As you start to turn back in towards your opponent, begin chambering the kicking leg (Figure 464) and, as the body once again lines up with your target, drive the kicking leg straight through, using the energy of the jump to generate the power required to strike with maximum force (Figure 465).

Fig 464 Chamber the kicking leg.

Fig 465 Strike the target with the correct striking part of the foot.

Fig 466 Working from a left lead in an angular stance ...

The Jumping Spinning Round Kick

This particular kick is a true jumping spinning kick in the fullest sense of the word, as the kicking leg travels in a circular motion from the starting point to the finishing point. A great deal of energy can be generated with this kick, as the body winds out of the spin. This is due to the momentum of the spin enabling the leg to travel at maximum velocity.

Working from a left lead in an angular stance (Figure 466), twist the body backwards in a clockwise direction, looking over your right shoulder as you do (Figure 467). From here, lift your right leg into the air (Figure 468) and jump as high as you can off your left leg (Figure 469). As your body starts to travel back round to the starting point, begin bringing your left kicking leg up into a chambered position and focus on the striking area of the target (Figure 470). Finally, drive the hips through to bring your body back round to the front, as you snap the kicking leg out towards its mark, striking with the instep or the ball of the foot (Figure 471).

Fig 467 ... twist your body backwards in a clockwise motion.

Fig 468 Bring your non-kicking leg high into the air.

Fig 469 Jump off your kicking leg.

Fig 470 Chamber the leg ready for the kick.

Fig 471 Strike the target with the correct striking part.

The Jumping Spinning Side Kick

The previous two kicks involved spinning backwards to generate the energy for the jump, however, with this one we'll focus on spinning forwards instead. As you may well find through your own investigations of the kicks, as you become more confident with them, when a spin is involved, there is normally more than one way of performing it. The jumping spinning side kick is a very versatile kick and can be performed with either a forwards spin or a simple backwards spin. The forwards spin in this demonstration has been used to give you a different perspective on how the spins may be performed.

From a left lead in more of an angular stance (Figure 472), drive the rear leg (your right leg) through to the front and use this movement to start the spinning process (Figure 473). Using the energy of projecting the rear leg forwards, jump off your left leg and continue to twist the body as you gain height (Figure 474). As you feel yourself cross the centre line, begin bringing the head round to once again focus on the target by looking over your left shoulder (Figure

161

475). Chamber the leg in readiness for the kick (Figure 476) and, once you have returned to a side-on position, drive the kicking leg straight through in the same way as you do for a static side kick, striking the target area with the heel or the blade of the foot (Figure 477).

Fig 472 Working from a left lead in an angular stance ...

Fig 473 ... bring your rear leg through to the front.

Fig 474 Jump off the kicking leg.

Fig 475 Twist the body in the air.

Fig 476 Chamber the kick.

Fig 477 Strike the target with the correct kicking part.

The Jumping Spinning Hook Kick

This is one of the all-time classic kicks and probably the one kick that is used the most in the martial arts movies by big kicking stars. It's an incredibly impressive kick; however, it is also an incredibly effective kick when used with speed and timing. The thing you may well find with jumping spinning kicks is that they look great in demonstrations, however, as previously mentioned, a lot of them can be a little ineffective when used under pressure or when in competition. The longer you spend jumping and spinning, the less chance you have of actually landing the kick and, although Tony Jaa made the 720-degree jumping spinning kick famous in the movie *Ong-Bak*, in the heat of the moment a simple 180-degree jumping spinning kick, such as this one, is more likely to find its mark.

From a left lead using an angular or side-on stance (Figure 478), keeping the feet where they are, twist the body in a clockwise motion as fast as you can and whip the head round to look over your right shoulder, in order to spot the target (Figure 479). At the same time, jump in the air as

high as you can and use the momentum of the first twist to generate the whipping motion required for this kick (Figure 480). As the body starts to come back round, begin chambering the leg in readiness for the kick (Figure 481) and, as the leg straightens out, hook it back in towards the target, using the heel or the flat of the foot as the striking tool (Figure 482).

The Jumping Spinning Back Kick

The jumping spinning back kick is the successor to the spinning back kick, as this is definitely the more advanced of the two kicks. Whereas it could be argued that the spinning back kick can deliver more power, the jumping version is certainly more versatile and, in some situations, faster. There are several different ways to perform a jumping spinning back kick and each way has its own unique advantages. Unfortunately, there just aren't enough pages in this book to show every possible way of performing each technique contained within. Therefore, we will learn the most efficient way of performing this kick, focusing on speed and power as opposed to distance.

Fig 478 In a left lead ...

Fig 479 ... twist the body in a clockwise motion.

Fig 480 Jump into the air, continuing the spin.

Fig 481 Chamber the leg.

Fig 482 Hook the leg through as the kick finds its mark.

Fig 483 In a left lead …

In a left lead working from an angular or side stance (Figure 483), bend the knees slightly to prepare the body for the jump (Figure 484). Jump into the air, bringing both feet off the ground at the same time (Figure 485). Twist the body approximately 90 degrees, so your back now faces the target, and chamber the leg in preparation for the kick (Figure 486). From this final position, drive the kicking leg back towards the target in a perfectly straight line and strike the mark with either the heel or the blade of the foot (Figure 487).

The Jumping Spinning Axe Kick
As with the jumping spinning back kick, the jumping spinning axe kick is another kick that, in the right situation, can be more effective than a static axe kick or indeed a spinning axe kick. Always try to follow the golden rule with the axe kick and use it to attack over the blind shoulder wherever possible (an explanation of the blind shoulder can be found in the axe kick section in Chapter 6) as there is a greater likelihood of the kick landing when used in this way. It is also a very

Fig 484 … bend the knees slightly.

Fig 485 Spring up high into the air.

Fig 486 Twist the body 90 degrees clockwise.

Fig 487 Stab the leg out in a completely straight line.

effective kick to use, as it can be quite awkward to defend against when done with speed and timing, due to the way the leg travels. From experience with this kick, a lot of fighters will duck into it, rather than lean away from it, so with a little time and practice, this could be a kick that is very effective for you.

Working from a left lead in an angular or side stance (Figure 488), bend the knees slightly to prepare for the jump (Figure 489). As you spring into the air, start turning your body for the spin and bring your head round to look over your right shoulder (Figure 490). As you start to come back round to the front once again, begin straightening out your leg, driving it up high into the air at the same time, to prepare for the kick (Figure 491). As it reaches its highest point, drive it straight down on to your opponent from above (Figure 492).

Fig 488 In a left lead ...

Fig 489 ... bend the knees slightly, to prepare for the jump.

Fig 490 Jump into the air and twist the body at the same time.

Fig 491 Straighten the kicking leg, driving it up above the target.

Fig 492 Drive it straight down on to the target in a vertical motion.

The Jumping Spinning Outside Crescent Kick

The final two kicks of this chapter use a semi-circular motion to generate their speed and power. Both kicks complement each other very well and allow for a quick attack, with the outside version, and a distance attack, with the inside version. They can also be used for more close-range attacks and, due to the way they travel, you may find the jumping spinning versions more effective to use than the simpler spinning versions covered earlier. As with the static kick version, the jumping spinning outside crescent kick uses the outside part of the foot to strike with, from where it derives its name.

From a left lead using an angular or side-on stance (Figure 493), prepare for the jump by slightly bending the knees (Figure 494). From this position, jump into the air as high as you can and twist the body round at the same time as you take off (Figure 495). As the body starts to come back round again, begin straightening out the leg, ensuring it remains on the same line as your target so as not to go over the top and miss altogether (Figure 496). Drive the kick through, using the

Fig 493 In a left lead …

Fig 494 … bend the knees slightly.

whole body combined with the spin to generate the power, and be sure to kick with the correct part of the foot (Figure 497).

Fig 495 Spring into the air and as you do twist the body at the same time.

Fig 496 Bring the leg round in a semi-circular motion.

Fig 497 Strike the target with the correct part of the foot.

The Jumping Spinning Inside Crescent Kick

This is the last kick in the chapter and finally brings the technical aspect of kickboxing to a close. The jumping spinning inside crescent kick is a great kick that can be used to attack the head or body with great speed and power. It can also be used to attack the guard and, although it might not be as effective as the static version for doing this, if used correctly it will still open up the opponent, allowing easier access to the head and body.

From a left lead, utilizing an angular or side-on stance (Figure 498), twist the body in a clockwise motion, keeping the feet where they are (Figure 499). As the twist reaches its maximum, begin bringing the rear (right) leg up into the air to assist the jump (Figure 500). As the rear leg starts to travel back towards the centre line, jump off the left leg and continue to travel clockwise with the energy generated from the spin (Figure 501). Ensuring the kicking leg travels along the same line as the mark you are targeting (in this case the head), begin to straighten the leg so that by the time it lands it is locked out fully and striking with the correct part of the foot (Figure 502).

Something to Think About
As your flexibility increases, you will start to see a change in your jumping, spinning and kicking

Fig 498 Starting in a left lead ...

Fig 499 ... twist the body in a clockwise motion.

Fig 500 Bring the rear leg off the floor.

Fig 501 Jump off the lead leg, continuing to spin.

Fig 502 Straighten the leg and drive the body round to complete the kick.

ability. Take the outside crescent kick as a great example. In the photos used for the breakdown, you can clearly see the rear, non-kicking leg moves into a more split-style position when in the air. This is quite commonly seen in the more flexible martial artists but will in no way add anything extra to the kick.

In the early stages of your jumping spinning kick training (and indeed your complete training for that matter), you will probably find that flexibility will be a key issue for you. I can't emphasize enough about the importance of developing this aspect of your training. That's not to say you should compromise your health and safety in the process, of course; that would be dangerous and have a completely reverse effect in the long term. However, when you first start out studying kickboxing, or indeed any form of martial art that involves kicking, if your flexibility isn't great, your kicks will be of a similar ilk.

Spending some quality time on your stretching will greatly assist your kicking ability. Where spinning kicks and jumping spinning kicks are involved, as your flexibility improves, so will your ability to perform these types of kicks. It is also a never-ending journey. Even when you have developed your flexibility, there is then the job of maintaining it. Admittedly this is somewhat less of a challenge than gaining your flexibility but it is still something that you will need to do. The simple rule, however, is 'anyone can be a world champion' – all you need to do is train like a world champion. This simply means that if you want something badly enough, all you need to do is, quite simply, 'whatever it takes to get it'. If the ability to perform incredible jumping spinning kicks is what you want, then put the time and effort into them and you will achieve this – but make sure you train the right thing in the right order.

Kickboxing is a demanding sport and in order to become good at it you need to train hard. Don't be one of the many that study it half-heartedly

and finally quit only to say 'it wasn't all that good'. It might not necessarily be the sport for you after all, but don't dismiss it until you have given it enough of your time to be able to give it a proper evaluation.

Consider some if the greatest kickboxers that have ever been. Fighters like Benny 'The Jet' Urquidez or Don 'The Dragon' Wilson, who have gone down in history for their kickboxing ability. These fighters and many more like them have taken kickboxing to the highest levels and exceeded in it. Their attitude towards their fighting and their dedication towards their training brought about the incredible successes they achieved in their careers and, had they adopted the attitude of so many others, we wouldn't be blessed with these incredible fighters today.

You get out of life what you put into it, and this goes for everything you do. Kickboxing has changed the lives of so many people all over the world and it's incredible to think that something that involves punching and kicking can do this. However, for those that look a little deeper, it's easy to see that there's much more to kickboxing than just this. The discipline, the dedication, the persistence, the commitment and all the other qualities and values that are needed to simply persevere with the study of the art, let alone excel in it, are incredible. What you find over time is that these simple values and qualities, if we understand them, can not only help us massively in our training, but are the same values and qualities that can also be used to help us in every other area of our lives.

It is for that reason that not only is kickboxing a great hobby for some, a route to health and wellbeing for others, a vehicle to help with weight loss for anyone seeking alternative methods and an overall incredible confidence-booster that also teaches you how to defend yourself – it also has the power to change our lives for the better. Who wouldn't want to study it?

11 Sparring Drills

When I first started out writing this book I hadn't planned on including a chapter on sparring drills. My initial intention was simply to show the technical aspects of kickboxing and introduce the reader to the many different hand and leg techniques contained within the art. From my experiences in the martial arts world, one thing has become very apparent. Today's student is different to the student of yesteryear. Sometimes for the better, but occasionally for the worse.

Martial arts have become very commercialized over the past few years and there are now a greater number of martial art schools and academies than ever before. It almost seems as if everyone is jumping on the bandwagon and students with very little experience are taking on the role of instructor and opening schools in order to share what knowledge they have with the rest of the world (or at least their local area).

This is great, providing the instructor has the knowledge to share; however, this isn't always the case and, unfortunately, if the instructor can't competently show something, then generally they don't. What this then tends to breed is a new type of student that only has a percentage of the knowledge they should have for their art and, as this student moves up to the role of instructor, the cycle starts again.

In time we may eventually end up with martial arts schools that only teach the basics, as that might be all the instructor knows or is able to show proficiently. While some might argue that this might not be a bad thing, I believe an instructor is doing the student an injustice if they are incapable of showing everything applicable to that art form, whether the student will ever use it or not. At least that way they then have the knowledge available to them and, therefore, the option to choose.

The term kickboxing is actually used to cover a wide range of fighting styles and many schools that have broken away from their traditional roots now choose this generic term in order to try and associate what they are teaching with a name that most potential students are familiar with. As such there are now many different styles of kickboxing out there, the most popular being freestyle, semi-contact and, of course, full contact.

When I first began writing this book, I wanted to try and capture as many of the techniques applicable to the many different styles of kickboxing available. In this way I believed I wouldn't alienate any particular version and would in turn allow the reader to experience as many techniques as possible. As the book progressed, and the content began to take form, it became apparent to me that I couldn't produce a book on kickboxing without this final chapter in it.

A technical book on kickboxing is all well and good, as it arms the reader with a huge number of hand and leg techniques that they can then develop for themselves with training drills to show them how to develop each technique even further. However, developing techniques in isolation in all honesty isn't enough. It would be like learning to drive a car without actually ever driving the car. This is where sparring comes in.

Sparring is the essence of any martial art, as it helps the student to develop their fighting ability. Not all martial arts call their sparring, sparring, however. For some of the non-sport-based fighting arts it is an opportunity to 'pressure test' the art; a term that is coined a lot with the reality-based art forms that are becoming quite popular. Regardless of what it is called, a fighting art isn't really a fighting art unless you are able to fight with it.

Sparring does just that, as it gives the student the ability to take all of their technical knowledge and ability, and put it into a semi-realistic environment for the street or a realistic environment for the sport, in order to see how they perform. I once heard Barry McGuigan refer to boxing as 'a physical game of chess'. This has been a phrase that has stuck with me throughout the whole of my martial arts training, as I believe it is a great way of summing up any fighting art. In chess, the skill is staying a few steps ahead of your opponent and knowing all the possible moves available to you, based on how your opponent reacts to your last move. In boxing, or rather kickboxing in our case, it's the same game, except ours is a bit more physical.

Having been a kickboxing instructor now for many years, I regularly see good-level students that can punch and kick a pair of focus pads with incredible speed, timing and power, get reduced back to that of a beginner once they enter the world of sparring. As the late great Bruce Lee once said, 'boards don't hit back' (*Enter the Dragon* 1973, Warner Brothers), and this is true to a lesser extent with focus pads (unless they are in the hands of a skilled pad-feeder, of course). Once you try to punch or kick a moving, defending target that has the ability to hit you back at the same time, the game changes completely and, if the game you're playing is full contact, then you need to be careful.

For this reason, I have decided to include a final 'bonus' chapter utilizing simple-to-perform sparring drills that can be trained with a sparring partner to help you make the transition from pad-puncher to kickboxer, so glove up and have some fun!

Sparring Equipment

Before you embark on your journey into the world of sparring, there are a few things you need to get in order to ensure that both you and your sparring partner are adequately protected from the punches and kicks that may land. Figure 503 shows the minimum requirement of sparring equipment required for kickboxing sparring training. Don't confuse this with the equipment required for competitive fighting, as in some cases the requirements are a lot less. In training, however, the more protection you can offer yourself and your partner, the better (and the more sensible).

For the head, you will need a good-quality head guard. There are many different styles, types and qualities available, and it is recommended that you go for the one that is likely to offer you the most protection for the level of contact you intend to apply.

For the teeth, you need a good-quality gum shield. Cheaper versions may well do the job and offer a degree of protection, however, it's worth paying a little more to save on the expense of dentistry bills, which will almost certainly be a lot more should the cheaper gum shields not be quite so good. You can purchase a gum shield from most sports shops or simply look on the internet. However, for a more professionally fitted one that can be moulded to fit your mouth exactly, then you will need to consult your dentist.

For the hands, a good-quality pair of boxing gloves is required that offers both hand protection

Fig 503 The minimum requirement of sparring equipment required for kickboxing sparring training.

to the wearer, as well as adequate padding to protect your partner from the contact that will be made – ideally, a closed glove, as opposed to a glove that allows the fingers or thumbs to protrude. The kickboxer tends not to need the fingers exposed, as there is no grappling involved; this will also prevent the possibility of a stray finger or thumb finding its way into the eye of your opponent.

For the male kickboxer, the groin certainly needs to be well-protected, particularly as this area will become exposed while kicking and is a readily available target for an accidental kick off your opponent. For this it is advisable to invest in a good-quality deluxe-style groin guard that offers complete protection. The cup-style groin guard will suffice and certainly be a cheaper option but, from experience, it doesn't offer as much protection against the big back-leg power kicks, should one accidently slip through.

Shin pads are another essential, although you can't see them in the photo, as these will protect you from a shin-on-shin clash or a shin-on-elbow clash, which can be very painful until your shins toughen up. It will also offer protection to your partner should you connect with an off-target round kick to the head, for example. As with all the sparring equipment, there are many different styles of shin pad available. It would be wise to consider a pad that covers the whole of the shin and one that won't move around as you train. The dipped-foam style of shin pads, for example, sometimes only cover the front of the shin and have a tendency to slip round, due to the fact that they don't absorb the sweat and instead sit on top of it creating a frictionless surface that moves through contact.

Footpads are the final essential and are designed solely for the protection of your partner. As the kick is generally more powerful than the punch, a good-quality pair of foot pads is recommended. Again there are pads that allow the toes and/or heel to remain exposed and there are pads that cover the whole foot. For kickboxing, you will need a footpad that covers the whole foot and, ideally, one made of leather or polyurethane, as these are generally considered to be the better of the range and less likely to split or tear.

Defences

Ideally, by this stage of the book you should understand how to punch and how to kick, and, if you have been training properly, you should by now be able to kick and punch a target in many different ways and at many different angles. Consequently, the first thing to focus on, where sparring is concerned, is the defences.

As sparring is a skill, you naturally improve in this area with the more training you dedicate to it, so to begin with start slowly and methodically. It is very easy to land a punch on someone who has never had to defend one before, so the attacker in these drills needs to take this into account and show respect to their opponent by not going full-on in the early stages.

Unlike in other fighting styles, kickboxing uses the arms a great deal to cover the vulnerable areas of your body, a bit like a shield would protect the body from an attack with a weapon. As the attacks in kickboxing are fast and furious, and normally involve a rapid flurry of techniques, it can be very difficult to block every single shot that is thrown. Consequently, the kickboxer utilizes more of a cover-and-move approach to their defence, rather than a stand-and-block approach. Be aware though that even the greatest fighter in the world will get hit, so don't be too downhearted if you don't defend against every attack that is thrown. Sometimes getting hit helps you to learn what it's like to get hit, so it's not such a shock when it happens for real.

Basic Defence Against a Jab or a Cross

This defence works well against a straight punch to the head area. From your fighting stance, simply bring the gloves together and in front of the head, as shown in Figure 504. For this to work effectively, you need to ensure that the gap between the arms is wide enough for you to see through, but not so wide that the punch can sneak through. You also need to slightly shrug the shoulders as the punch lands in order to cushion the neck and prevent the whiplash effect that a straight punch can sometimes cause, as the head is snapped back due to the force of the blow, particularly if you are a little slow in getting your guard up.

Fig 504 Defence against a jab or cross.

Fig 505 Defence against a body hook.

Fig 506 Defence against a hooking
punch to the head.

Fig 507 Defence against an uppercut.

Basic Defence Against a Body Hook

A body hook can be a devastating blow, so your defence here needs to be tight. If you hold your guard correctly, you shouldn't have to move the arms very much, so most of the time this area should be naturally covered. As the punch comes in, simply place the elbow of your defending arm on your hip and ensure the fist of the same arm resides on your chin, as shown in Figure 505. To achieve this position you will need to curl the body slightly; however, this action actually helps in absorbing the energy of the punch. The same defence can be used for a hook to the other side.

Basic Defence Against a Hook Punch to the Head

This time you are going to bring the defending arm up to the head, so your hand comes around to the back of the neck and your arm defends the blow, as shown in Figure 506. The motion of grabbing the neck with your gloved hand will ensure that the whole of the side of the head is covered, should the punch be long, and also will ensure that the gap between your bicep and forearm isn't wide enough for the hook to sneak through.

Basic Defence Against an Uppercut

Due to the direction that the uppercut travels and its intended target, the most effective defence for this attack is to bring the gloves together and the elbows down low towards the mid-line, as shown in Figure 507. Ensure the elbows are brought tightly together to prevent the punch from slipping through the middle of your arms and make sure the head is also well protected by the gloves. Also ensure you can still see where the punch is at all times and, most importantly, where the next punch is coming from.

Basic Defence Against a Front Kick to the Body

One of the most effective forms of defence against a front kick is to follow the same line of defence as used for an uppercut, particularly if the attack is to the body, which it often is with this kind of kick. The kick can also be more powerful than the

Fig 508 Defence against a front kick.

uppercut, so ensure your guard is held tight, as shown in Figure 508, in order to prevent the kick powering its way through and finding the mid-line, even though your guard was there.

Basic Defence Against a Side Kick to the Body

This defence gives you a different option should you find yourself in a more side-on or angled stance, and can, in fact, be more effective than the previous defence, as there is less likelihood of the kick powering its way through your guard. It also works well against any straight kick to the body, so it is a good one to practise for the inevitable occasion when you are recovering from a kick and your opponent counter-attacks. Keeping your rear hand on your chin as normal, bring your lead hand in a downward motion, as if you are trying to bring your elbows together (Figure 509). The actual blocking area for this defence is the elbow or the tricep of your lead arm. Keep the arms in position until you are safely out of range of a second attack or until your opponent lands the foot.

Fig 509 Defence against a side kick.

Fig 510 Defence against a round kick to the head.

Fig 511 Defence against an axe kick.

Fig 512 Parry against a straight punch to the head.

Basic Defence Against a Round Kick to the Head

The most effective defence for this attack is identical to the defence used for the hooking punch. As the attack is targeting the side of the head, simply bring your blocking arm up, so you grab the back of the neck, and absorb the kick using the arm, as shown in Figure 510.

Basic Defence Against an Axe Kick

If done properly, the axe kick can be a difficult kick to defend against. If the attack is a little slow and lacks power, then you can bring the lead hand up, shielding your head, as shown in Figure 511. The only thing to be careful with when adapting this defence is that, if the kick does have some power behind it, it may well drive your guard down, leaving you vulnerable to a follow-up attack. To counter this, you can try stepping in with the defence as the kick reaches its highest point, which can not only absorb the attack but also has the tendency to throw the attacker off-balance. When defending against an axe kick, the most effective form of defence is to lean or step back out of the way, keeping the chin covered by the lead shoulder.

Basic Parry Against a Straight Punch to the Head

The parry is a popular and very effective form of defence, particularly when used with movement. It won't always stop the most powerful of attacks, if the attack moves into the parry, as shown in the next drill, but if the attack travels in a straight line, then the parry can be quite effective. As the attacker throws the punch (in this case a jab), slip the head to the side and, using whichever hand is nearest to the attacking area at the time, attempt to intercept the attack and push it off-target (Figure 512).

Basic Parry Against a Round Kick to the Head

This can be an effective defence against a freestyle attack (one that doesn't deliver a full-contact blow) but, if the round kick is travelling at full power, it might be wise to cover the area using your arms as a shield, instead of trying to parry it, particularly as the parry might not be strong enough to stop the force of the blow. As the kick approaches the target, slip the head to the side and bring the opposite hand into the line of attack, in an attempt to stop the kick in its tracks or push it off-target (Figure 513).

Training Drills

As you can see from the previous examples, there is more than one way of defending against an attack because there is more than one way that you can be attacked. The main attacks in kickboxing fall into seven main categories:

1. Straight attack to the head – as in the case of the jab and the cross, for example.
2. Straight attack to the body – as in the case of the front kick, side kick, spinning back kick and so on.
3. Circular attack to the head – as in the case of the hooking punches, the elbows, the round kick, the hooking kick, the crescent kick, the spinning hook kick and so on.
4. Circular attack to the body – as in the case of the hooking punch, the round kick, the spinning round kick and so on.

Fig 513 Parry against a kick to the head.

5. Ascending attack to the head – as in the case of the uppercut, the rising elbow strike, the side kick and so on.
6. Ascending attacks to the body – as in the case of the uppercut.
7. Descending attacks to the head – as in the case of the axe kick.

Consequently, the same techniques can be used to defend against any attack that travels in the same direction as the ones used in the previous examples, that is the defence used to cover the head from a hooking punch will also work against a spinning hook kick, as the kick travels along the same line of attack as the hooking punch.

In order for these defences to work effectively, you must practise them through repetition. With your sparring equipment on, work through the various defences covered above, in isolation, as detailed below.

Defences in Isolation

Have your partner throw the jab and, from your front-on fighting stance, bring your arms up to cover against the attack, as shown in Figure 504. After each punch, instruct your partner to pause as you reset your guard and then, when you are ready, they throw the second jab and so on. Continue for two minutes before changing to the next technique. Once you become confident defending against the basic attacks, try adding in more advanced attacks. For example, replace the hooking punch to the body with a spinning round kick to the body and see how the same defence works against this technique. You can also instruct your partner to make the attack more realistic, so they get to practise their explosive speed and targeting ability, while you get to practise your defence against a full speed, targeted attack.

Attack and Defend

For this drill, you begin the attack and your partner defends. They then attack back and you defend. The attack back can either be instant, which will help develop your reactions and timing, or it can be delayed, enabling you to work on your concentration, as you will need to stay alert to prevent being hit.

A slightly more advanced version of this drill can be done using a three-beat rhythm, which involves you attacking, your partner attacking and then you attacking again. You then switch the roles on the next go, so that your partner attacks, you attack and your partner attacks. Alternatively, you can work the same drill with a partner holding a pair of focus pads. This time you attack the pads and they return the attack using the focus pads to hit with, which you then hit again with your counter-strike – you jab the focus pad, your partner simulates a jab by attacking off their lead hand with a focus pad, which you then defend, and as they draw the pad back for you to target, you attack the same pad with a jab once again.

Once you are confident with this drill using single attacks, try adding in multiple attacks, so you might attack with a jab and a cross, and your partner returns with a jab and a cross. You might attack with a jab, cross, hook, round kick and your partner attacks back with the same combination. Alternatively, you can combine this same drill into a three-beat rhythm, as before.

Defend and Attack

This training drill works in the same way as the previous drill except this time you receive the attack first and then you follow with the counter-attack. This drill gets you used to being attacked, defending and straight away attacking back. Ideally, there should be no pause in-between defending the attack and counter-attacking.

Attack Defend Attack

This time you attack and your partner defends, instantly returning with a counter-attack, which you defend. As soon as you have covered the attack, you explode back with a multiple-attack combination. This particular drill works well when your partner holds a pair of focus pads, as you can explode into the pads with full power. Combinations to consider are:

1. jab, cross, jab;
2. cross, hook, cross;
3. hook, cross, hook;
4. hook, uppercut, hook;
5. uppercut, hook, uppercut.

Defend Attack Defend

The final drill simply works along the same lines as the previous one, except this time you receive an attack first, then you attack and, finally, your partner explodes back with a multiple-attack combination, which you can either defend against or hold pads for.

Free-Play

Finally for this section, you can attack with any single technique and your partner defends and counters with any single technique. Isolate the hands only, utilizing any hand attack to start with, then the legs only and finally attack with either a hand or a leg attack in any order. Once comfortable with this drill, add in multiple attacks (two, three or four) in the same way.

Evade and Counter Drills

Defending an attack by absorbing the blow can be an effective way to avoid being hit, however, some might argue that to a lesser degree you are still receiving a percentage of the hit, albeit indirectly. Consequently, a more effective method of defending against an attack is by avoiding the attack altogether. This takes a little more skill and training, and requires a high degree of timing, but with practice it can be very effective, particularly when you combine the evasion with a counter-attack at the same time. There are numerous ways of avoiding an attack. These include popular phrases such as bob and weave, slipping, leaning and rolling; all these really refer to is the movement of the body while carrying out the evasion.

The training drills that follow use various methods of evasion and counter techniques to avoid being hit, while at the same time landing your kicks and punches as efficiently and as effectively as possible.

Evade and Counter Against a Straight Punch

Square up to your opponent in your fighting stance (Figure 514). As your opponent starts their attack, using either a jab or cross punch, transfer your body weight on to your rear leg and lean back out of the way to avoid being hit. At the same time,

chamber your kicking leg for a side-kick attack to the mid-line (Figure 515). When the punch reaches full extension or, as you see the mid-line open up, stab out the side kick as fast as you can to the open area (Figure 516). The advantage of this evasion and counter is that, as you transfer your body weight on to your rear leg, you naturally lean back to assist with the weight transfer, which in turn automatically moves the head out of the line of attack. This movement creates the distance required to effectively execute a mid-section side kick, which in turn prevents a potential follow-up attack from your opponent as the leg, which is longer than the arm, creates a natural barrier between you and your partner.

Evade and Counter Against a Straight Punch 2

Square up to your opponent in your fighting stance (Figure 517). As your partner jabs, slip to the side by zoning out with your rear leg. Be sure to keep the chin tucked well behind the lead shoulder as you move, just in case (Figure 518).

Fig 514 Square-off with your opponent.

Fig 515 As your opponent attacks, lean back and chamber the leg.

Fig 516 Strike the exposed area with a side kick.

From here flow straight into a lead leg round kick to the mid-section, being careful not to hit the rear arm, which, if held properly, should be protecting the right side of your opponent's body. It is also possible, when using this style of attack, to strike with the ball of the foot, particularly for smaller target areas or for a deeper penetration of the kick (Figure 519).

Fig 517 Square-off with your opponent.

Fig 518 Slip the punch.

Fig 519 Round kick to the body.

Fig 520 Square-off with your opponent.

Fig 521 Slip the punch.

Fig 522 Round kick to the body.

Figures 520–522 show the same evade and counter from a different angle.

Evade and Counter Against a Straight Punch 3

Square up to your opponent in your fighting stance (Figure 523). As your partner jabs, transfer your body weight on to your rear leg to lean out of the way of the attack but this time remain more front-on. As your body weight transfers to your rear leg, chamber the front leg in readiness for a front kick (Figure 524). As the mid-line of your opponent opens up, stab out the kick, striking with the ball of the foot (Figure 525). As with the side kick, the front kick can also be a great stopping kick, if done correctly.

Evade and Counter Against a Straight Punch 4

For the final drill at this level, we'll counter with a straight punch to the body. This counter can be a little riskier and does involve a good understanding of timing but it also keep us closer in to our opponent, allowing for a good combination of punches with which to follow. Square up to your opponent as before (Figure 526). As your partner throws the jab, slip underneath the punch to avoid

the attack and to bring you in line with the body (Figure 527). Be sure to keep the chin tucked

Fig 523 Square off with your opponent.

Fig 524 Lean back and chamber the leg.

Fig 525 Front kick to the exposed area.

tightly behind the lead shoulder and the rear arm tight against the body and chin, just in case of a lead round kick or hook punch from your opponent. As you drop to avoid the attack, stab out your jab to the mid-line of your partner, as they open up the body (Figure 528). From here you can step in with a rear uppercut to finish.

Intermediate-Level Drills

As previously mentioned, repetition is the key to these drills, particularly to help you develop timing, a skill that enables us to beat our opponent to the attack, or simply to help us avoid being hit altogether. These drills will also help you to develop the ability to read when your opponent is about to attack (known as telegraphing the technique), which is a vital skill if we want to defend or evade successfully. Train the previous drills with either one person attacking for a set period of time (between two and five minutes) or alternating the drill one for one. Once you have mastered the evasions against a straight attack, try your hand at these next ones.

Fig 526 Square-off with you opponent.

Fig 527 Slip the punch.

Fig 528 Jab to the body.

Evade and Counter a Circular Attack

Square up to your opponent (Figure 529). This time, your partner throws a rear hooking punch to the head. As they do, roll underneath it and ready the rear hand for a mid-line hook to the body (Figure 530). As you roll under the punch, drive your rear hooking punch into the mid-line of your opponent with the whole weight of your body behind it (Figure 531). As you roll back into your guard, attack with a lead hook to the chin over the top of your opponent's rear arm (Figure 532). The beauty of this one is that it uses the natural movement of the roll to set up the counter punch to the body and as the first punch stuns the opponent, the second punch finishes the job.

Evade and Counter a Straight Punch

Square up to your opponent (Figure 533). As your partner throws a cross punch, slip to the outside to avoid the attack and keep your rear hand firmly in place to avoid a follow up attack while at the same time moving the lead hand into place for an uppercut (Figure 534). As the cross from your opponent reaches full extension, strike the chin using your lead uppercut and twist the body into

the punch to generate the energy required for the knockout (Figure 535).

Fig 529 Square-off with your opponent.

Fig 530 Roll under the punch.

Fig 531 Rear hook to the body.

Fig 532 Lead hook to the head.

Fig 533 Square-off with your opponent.

Fig 534 Slip the punch.

Fig 535 Lead uppercut to the chin.

Evade and Counter a Straight Punch

This final drill involves a considerable amount of timing in order to pull it off. However, if you can invest some quality time in developing it, it is very effective. The evasion simply involves you executing a jumping spinning back kick, using the breakdown featured in Chapter 10. As your opponent attempts the attack, you simply jump, spin and kick to the mid-section, as they expose their mid-line. It is this movement that assists in the evasion of the attack, while at the same time countering with the back kick, as shown in Figure 536. If possible, another piece of safety equipment you could consider to assist with the development of this and similar drills is body armour. Body armour is used in a variety of martial arts in both competitive fighting and training form, in order to reduce the risk of injury to the mid-section from powerful, full contact attacks.

Advanced Sparring Drills

This final section will help you to develop the mentality of using multiple shots when attacking,

Fig 536 As your partner punches, perform a jumping spinning back kick to the exposed area.

instead of trying to rely on a single shot to do the job. Rarely will you find a single attack to be more effective than a multiple attack, particularly when sparring with an experienced fighter. The general rule when attacking is to set up the final blow with a rapid combination of well-executed attacks, in order to stun and disorientate your opponent, forcing them into making a mistake and leaving an open target for you to land a well-timed finishing shot.

Of course it doesn't always happen quite so easily as this, but to emphasize the point, it is often considered that by using a ten-hit combination as an example, the first few attacks would be blocked, the next few attacks would be evaded and the last few attacks would find their mark. This is certainly a more reliable method of attacking than just relying on a single shot each time. The last three drills will focus on some two-hit multiple-kicking attacks to train and develop, which will in turn help to develop your kicking ability and at the same time help you to understand the way you should be thinking when instigating the attack on your opponent.

The Double Round Kick Combo

In this drill, your intention is to land a round kick to your opponent's well-guarded head, by using your first kick to draw their guard down. Square-up to your opponent in your fighting stance as normal (Figure 537). Step up and attack to the body with your first kick (Figure 538). As you attack this area, the natural thing for your opponent to do is to bring their guard down slightly to cover the attack and to prevent the kick from landing to the body. This manoeuvre should be just enough to expose the head and give you a large enough target to land your second kick. As soon as your first kick lands, and you see their guard drop, re-chamber the leg (Figure 539) and attack back up to the head, as fast as possible (Figure 540). If done quickly enough, you should find that your opponent doesn't have enough time to react to the second kick and, therefore, shouldn't be able to bring their guard back up again in time to stop the second kick from landing.

The key with this attack is obviously speed and timing. Generally, if you hit to the body and your

Fig 537 Square-off with your opponent.

Fig 538 Round kick to the body to bring the guard down.

Fig 539 Chamber the leg.

Fig 540 Round kick to the exposed head.

balance allows, then firing the kick straight back up to the head without putting the foot down should, in the majority of cases, find a target. It is also advisable to keep the knee high, when you chamber the leg, in preparation for the second kick, as this will help your balance, speed and timing. If you drop the knee, then you will have to use valuable time in bringing it back up again, which in turn uses valuable energy and could result in the opponent getting their guard back up quicker than you can kick.

The Hook Kick Round Kick Combo
This drill relies on your ability to fool your opponent and is a great combination to work against the counter fighter. As with all multiple-kicking combinations, your intention is to set up the second kick by using an initial kick that leads your opponent into a false sense of security. Just when they think the danger is over, you use their overconfidence to your advantage and, providing your speed and timing is good, then it's quite possible that you get the head shot with the second kick.

Square-up to your opponent in your fighting stance as normal (Figure 541). Execute a hook kick using your lead leg and target the head of your opponent (Figures 542–545). If the kick happens to land, then you have achieved your goal with just one attack. If, however, your opponent evades your hook kick by leaning back or moving their head out of the way, then without landing the leg from your first kick, simply chamber the leg once more as it passes the centre line of your opponent and fire out the round kick as your opponent moves to counter your attack (Figure 546).

Sparring owes a lot to speed and timing and, in most cases, the faster you are and the better your timing, the greater your advantage. The timing element is important because even if your opponent is quicker than you, providing you can time your attack just right, you can still beat them to the shot. Put this to the test by instructing your partner to try and land a jab to your body as you attempt to land the round kick, and see who is more successful. Just be sure you are wearing your head guard if you attempt this drill, as with speed often comes power.

Fig 541 Square-off with your opponent.

Fig 542 Chamber the leg for a hooking kick.

Fig 543 Hooking kick to the head.

Fig 544 Take the leg past the centre line.

Fig 545 Chamber the leg.

Fig 546 As the opponent attempts to counter, round kick to the head.

Axe Kick Side Kick Combo

This final combination is one that can be incredibly effective, providing you can spend some time developing it. The beauty of an axe kick is that it can be very difficult to defend against. Plus, as it does require a good level of flexibility in order to perform to any reasonable degree, it isn't a kick that you see performed all that often; particularly as not everyone has the discipline to develop their flexibility to the required degree. Therefore, when you are sparring against an opponent that isn't used to dealing with an axe kick, the chances are that they will not be that proficient in defending against it. Even if they are quick enough to get out of the way, most of the time they will duck right into its path, so it finds its mark anyway.

With this particular combination, we will assume your opponent decides to try and block the kick instead of trying to evade it, which allows us to utilize the side kick more effectively. Square-off with your opponent in your fighting stance (Figure 547). Execute the axe kick, using your lead leg and bringing the kick up as high as you can (Figure 548). This practice of bringing the kick up high will ensure your attack clears the blind shoulder and, at the same time, allows you to drop the kick directly down on to your opponent, reducing the chances of them blocking it with any real effect. The only thing you need to be careful of with an axe kick is kicking too slowly, as this will give an opponent time to rush forwards and knock you off-balance; so, as you attack with this kick, be sure to attack as fast as you can.

In this instance your opponent brings their lead arm up in an attempt to block the kick and, as they do, two things can now happen: either the power of your kick drives the block down and out of the way; or you simply bounce the axe kick off the guard. Either way, once the axe kick has prepared the way for the second kick, chamber the leg (Figure 549) and, providing there is still an open target due to your partner attempting to block the first kick, fire out a side kick to the mid-line (Figure 550).

Fig 547 Square-off with your opponent.

Fig 548 Axe kick off the lead leg.

Fig 549 Chamber the leg without landing the kick.

Fig 550 Side kick to the exposed area.

The other option with this combination is to bounce the axe kick off the body of your opponent in order to disorientate them and, hopefully, cause them to panic, open up their guard and present the mid-line for the side kick. This second version works well if they don't try to block the kick and instead lean backwards instead of ducking. Most of the time when you lean out of the way of an axe kick, your lead shoulder rises and acts as a natural defence against an attack of this type. Instead of wasting the axe kick, you can instead hit the body or shoulder with it and use it to set up a second attack, as described.

There are thousands of drills, combinations and ways of developing your kickboxing techniques, as well as your sparring ability, and this is probably a great topic for a second book. Until then, this final chapter will hopefully give you a starting point with which to take everything you have learned so far and put it into practice in a realistic sport-combat situation against a real-life opponent. As previously mentioned, sparring is a great way of honing your kickboxing skills and is a vital part of kickboxing training. Although you can still have a great deal of fun learning the technical aspect of kickboxing, it is not until you are trying to hit a moving target, that is also trying to hit you back, that you will fully appreciate or even understand exactly how it all works.

Regardless of your age, level and ability, kickboxing is a great sport, hobby or past-time and is one of very few activities you can do that will not only get you fit, healthy and help you to stay active, but could also one day save your life. So remember to train hard and train safely, keep yourself protected at all times and, above all, enjoy it and have some fun!

Index